Phil Shaw is a 29-year-old hi-stakes poker playe from London, England. He specialises in high-s $5/10-$25/50 no-limit hold'em cash games, $30/6u-ψ_ games, $200-$2000 sitngos and hi-stakes online and occasional live ιω_ naments. He discovered online poker whilst trying (and failing) to watch the Bruce Willis film *The Jackal* on television in April 2002 and opened his first poker account in that name. He has been known by variations of it ever since, including 'Jackal69' on PokerStars and 'Jackal78' on Full Tilt Poker.

He graduated Keble College, Oxford University in 2003 with a BA in English Language and Literature and currently writes for a variety of poker publications including *Inside Poker* and *Poker Player* by Dennis Publishing, and is a Guest Pro on poker video instructional site CardRunners.com alongside superstar online players like Brian Townsend and Taylor Caby, specialising in sitngo and mixed game tuition. He is also an avid teacher of the game through private coaching and believes that whilst poker is a game where luck plays its part, it can be overcome by anyone who has dedication and discipline and turned into a profitable hobby or even profession. His largest single win to date is around $76,000 in an online multi-table tournament.

Poker books from D&B

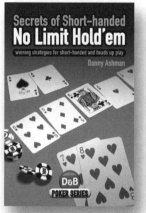

Secrets of Sit'n'gos

winning strategies for single-table poker tournaments

Phil Shaw

www.dandbpoker.com

First published in 2008 by D & B Publishing

Copyright © 2008 Phil Shaw

Reprinted 2009 twice, 2010

British Library Cataloguing-in-Publication Data
A catalogue record for this book is available from the British Library.

ISBN: 978-1-904468-43-1

All sales enquiries should be directed to:
D & B Publishing
Tel: (+44) 1273 711443
e-mail: info@dandbpoker.com
Website: www.dandbpoker.com

Cover design by Horatio Monteverde
Printed and bound in the US by Versa Press

Contents

Introduction 13

What is a sitngo? 13

Why play sitngos? 14

How much money can I expect to make? 14

1 Pre-Game Strategies 16

Prepare yourself 16

Game selection 16

Assessing your opponents 17

Structure implications 18

Turbo vs. standard speed sitngos 21

How much should you expect to pay in entry fees? 22

A note on multi-tabling sitngos 23

2   Other Considerations   24

Introducing position   24

Introducing hand ranges   25

Introducing EV (Expected Value)   26

Introducing ICM (the Independent Chip Model)   26

Harnessing the power of ICM   31

3   The Early Game   32

Introducing the early game   32

How well do you 'play poker'?   32

Playable hands in the early game   33

What type of game are you in?   37

Limping vs. raising   39

Playing in the blinds   40

Calling raises, reraising and moving all-in   41

ICM considerations for early game play   42

How your strategy changes as your chip stack increases   45

How your strategy changes if your chip stack decreases   45

Thoughts on tight vs. loose play in the early game   46

Postflop play in the early stages of sitngos   47

4   The Middle Game   51

Introducing the middle game   51

Introducing effective stack sizes   51

How preflop hand selection alters as your
    stack size diminishes   52

A note on blind stealing in sitngos   53

A note on the size of your opening raise as the blinds
    increase   53

Reraising and flat calling a raise in the middle game   *54*

Being reraised   *56*

ICM considerations for middle game play   *56*

Defending the blinds   *57*

5   The Late Game   *59*

Introducing the late game   *59*

The all-in zone   *59*

Playable hands in the late game   *61*

Assigning hand ranges to all-in players   *65*

Playing against limpers and limping with high blinds   *67*

ICM considerations for late game play   *68*

A note on antes   *69*

6   The Bubble   *71*

Introducing the bubble   *71*

The sitngo player's dilemma – hang on for third or play
to win?   *72*

ICM considerations for bubble play   *72*

Moving all-in on the bubble   *74*

A note on assuming optimal opposition, and
accounting for suboptimal opposition   *76*

Assessing stack sizes, blind structures and seating
positions   *76*

When all stacks are similar in size   *77*

When you have a dominating stack   *79*

When one of your opponents has a dominating stack   *81*

When you have a short stack or micro-stack   *82*

Attacking your nearest rivals   *83*

Calling all-in (and calling an all-in) on the bubble   84

Cooperative vs. non-cooperative bubble strategies   86

Manipulating all-in situations when players are
     short-stacked   87

Planning for and manipulating blind increases   89

When the stacks are still deep on the bubble   90

Playing a dominating stack when deep   90

Playing a medium stack when deep   91

7   In the Money (playing three-handed)   93

Introducing the money stages   93

Re-evaluating the payout structure   93

ICM considerations for three-handed play   94

Re-evaluating your strategy for three-handed play   95

When the stacks are still deep in three-handed play   96

8   Heads-Up (playing one-on-one)   98

Introducing heads-up play   98

Playing in a cash game freezeout   98

Smallball vs. jam or fold strategies   99

Playing smallball   99

Jam or fold   100

9   Strategies for Non-Standard Sitngos   104

Six-max sitngos   104

Two-table sitngos   107

Sitngo satellites with only one prize   109

Sitngo satellites with more than one prize   109

Making your own assessments of non-standard sitngo
    structures   *110*

When a level is determined by number of hands rather
    than time   *111*

A note on button movement when a player is eliminated   *111*

10   Miscellaneous Topics   *113*

The limitations of ICM   *113*

Other ICM considerations   *117*

Sitngo tools and resources   *118*

Bankroll considerations based on ROI and variance   *120*

Moving up!   *124*

From $200 to $100,000 in one year (and 5000 sitngos)   *125*

Rakeback   *128*

The future of sitngos   *130*

11   Sitngo Quizzes   *131*

Introducing the quiz section   *131*

The early game   *132*

The middle game   *153*

The late game   *169*

The bubble   *181*

In the money (playing three-handed)   *202*

Heads-up (one-on-one)   *208*

Non-standard sitngos   *219*

Introduction

What is a sitngo?

A sitngo is a poker tournament that, as the name suggests, begins as soon as the required number of players have registered, and as with all tournaments pays players based on their finishing positions according to a pre-advertised payout structure. Whereas most regular multi-table poker tournaments begin at a specific time and can accommodate a large number of players, a sitngo is designed to fulfil the needs of players who want their poker action immediately or with only a small waiting period. With the large numbers of players now taking part in them online this will often mean only seconds or minutes on the largest sites.

This demand has also led to diversity in the types of sitngo that are available. The standard format is a full table of 9-10 players but you can now also play six-max and one-on-one (heads-up) games, or multi-table formats catering for between 18 and 180 players. Similarly, there are different options available in terms of the speed of the sitngo with most sites offering 'standard' speed games with blind levels of 6-10 minutes and 'turbo' games where the levels are usually five minutes or less. For the purposes of this book we will be looking mostly at the one table no-limit hold'em format with 9-10 player games and a 50%/30%/20% payout structure for the top three players since this is by far the most popular. However, other formats are addressed in the section 'Strategies for non-standard sitngos'.

Why play sitngos?

Since the rise of internet poker, new players have had an unprecedented amount of choice over the games and formats they can play at the click of a button. So, why should someone who is just starting out in poker choose to play no-limit hold'em sitngos? As you will realise by reading this book there are many reasons, both from a practical and a strategic perspective.

If you are new to poker, sitngos will give you the opportunity to experience a number of different poker situations without the risks or the frustration of other formats. You will get to experience playing with deep stacks similar to cash games at the start for a fixed buy-in, but with around one-third of the players in an event getting paid you will experience far less frustration and variance than you will in multi-table tournaments. And as players are eliminated you will get to experience short-handed and (if you make it) heads-up play cheaply, which will also be good preparation should you ever make the final table of a large multi-table tournament.

As the sitngo progresses, the quickly rising blinds will allow you to employ some basic winning strategies to beat your opponents that can be easily learnt, as well as a few more expert ones that many players are not aware of which will increase your profit even more. They are also an efficient way for players on a limited bankroll to increase it quickly as is discussed in the chapter 'Bankroll considerations based on ROI and variance' on page 120. The question most players are interested in hearing the answer to however is 'how much money can I expect to make?' which we will turn to now.

How much money can I expect to make?

As with all things in poker, the amount of money you can expect to make is to a large extent dependent on the amount you are prepared to risk, and with sitngos regularly available online with buy-ins ranging from a few cents to over $5000 there is plenty of scope for choice and moving up the ladder as you progress. They also offer an excellent risk/reward proposition and so players starting out at the lower buy-ins can expect a healthy return and to rise quickly through the ranks as a consequence of this.

In sitngos profit is typically measured in terms of Return on Investment

(ROI), which refers to the amount of money you expect to make on average as a percentage of the overall cost of the event (i.e. the buy-in plus the entry fee). So, if a player in a $210+$15 sitngo has a 10% ROI they are making an average of $22.50 per sitngo. This is certainly a realistic return for the best players in the mid-level games with buy-ins of $100-$499, with the maximum realistic return tending up towards 15% for the lower stakes where there are many weak players, and down towards 5% for the higher stakes where there are often many expert players in each.

Also, since sitngo play becomes quite straightforward in the late stages there is good scope for multi-tabling them and combining a high ROI with high volume, for one of the best money-making propositions available in poker. Some players routinely manage to play hundreds of games per week (and as many as 16 simultaneously), with the highest stakes and highest-volume players making well into six figures on an annual basis from sitngos alone.

As an illustration of what is achievable by a dedicated player you should refer to the section 'From $200 to $100,000 in one year (and 5000 sitngos)' on page 125, where the progress of a player with a $200 bankroll is considered according to standard assumptions about achievable win rates and bankroll considerations. As the title of this section suggests, it is more than possible to go from very little to a great deal in a short period of time, although this will certainly take a lot of hard work and study.

Chapter One

Pre-Game Strategies

Prepare yourself

Tempting as it is to just jump into the first sitngo you see available there are a number of considerations and exercises that both beginning and expert players can benefit from to significantly increase their return. It should go without saying that if you want to make money playing poker then you should be focused, positive and lucid when you sit down to play (and not tired, upset, drunk or negative). However, here we will discuss those areas that specifically relate to sitngo play.

Game selection

One of the most overlooked aspects of sitngo play, even by experts, is game selection, and as you move up the stakes (or if you are only a small winner) it will become more and more important to discriminate in terms of what line-ups you will and won't play against. The factors you should take into consideration when selecting suitable games include your own ROI and that of the other players registered, the registration fee, and the volume that you wish to achieve.

For example, consider two 10-player sitngos, a $50+$5 and a $500+$25, and two players both of whom are among the best at their given level. Although at the lower limit a player is paying proportionally twice as much in fees as a higher limit player, it will usually be correct for him to be less discriminating simply because his skill edge against the average field is much greater, and his net profit per game is smaller. By contrast, a high stakes player may have no edge at all if the field is made up of tough regulars, but will be able to make a much higher amount per game when there are weak players registered.

In practical terms you will do well to look for sitngos with at least 2-3 bad or mediocre players registered as a rule of thumb at whatever stakes you play. At the lowest stakes (below $100) you should naturally find games with many of these players, so very little game selection will be required (and you will probably not recognise many players due to the size of the player pool). However at mid-stakes ($100-$499) you will need to start watching out for games in which many regulars are registered and avoid them, and at high stakes ($500+) you will need to be very focused on looking for games where there are weaker players registered if you want to achieve a healthy profit.

Assessing your opponents

As you play any sitngo you will want to be assessing your opponents in order to determine how they might behave as the blinds get higher, but it is also important to make judgements about them before even registering for the tournament. The best way of doing this at present is through sites like Sharkscope.com[1]. This is a datamining website which tracks sitngo results on all of the popular sites and allows users to look up their opponents' statistics to see whether they are winners or not. It provides information and graphs on areas such as number of games played, total and average profit, and average buy-in and ROI.

Non-subscribers are allowed five free searches a day, (which may be the best option unless you are a heavy-duty player). However, if you do sub-

---

[1] But note that PokerStars have recently banned use of this program whilst you are playing, and you should check with your site's terms and conditions if in doubt.

scribe there are a number of advanced features available that let you explore players more deeply by filtering according to specific game types, limit, speed or sitngo, stakes and entries. This can be useful in trying to figure out if a player's stats have been skewed by certain factors, for example if they have played a small number of hi-stakes heads-up matches.

However, the most important stats to pay attention to when 'sharkscoping' players are the basic ones. A reliable sample size for sitngo results is at least 1000 games at a certain level (or similar ones, as most players move up in stakes before completing this many games at one level) which should give a very accurate idea of a player's overall performance. However, a lot of players will not have this many games recorded so you will need to try and assess as best you can whether you want to compete against them. For example, if they are losing significantly over a few hundred games then that is a good sign, but if they have played less than a hundred and are around the breakeven point it will be hard to say.

You should also try to infer things from the other statistics on offer that will help you. For example, a player with an average buy-in of $11 registered for a $109 sitngo may be out of his depth or trying to move up in limits and may play tighter, and someone who has lost the last few games they played might make more mistakes. Most of this is easily assessable from the graphs provided which chart things like total profit according to games played and number of sitngos played at each level, and trying to interpret this information should increase your understanding of your opponents even more.

Structure implications

One of the most important factors in determining your potential edge in sitngos is the structure of the game. Depending on how many big blinds you begin with, how quickly the blinds rise and how long each level lasts, your edge may vary dramatically. It is therefore imperative that you investigate this before playing if you are unfamiliar with a site, are trying a new format or are just new to sitngos. The highest volume sites (currently PokerStars and Full Tilt Poker) generally have good structures, but on others you should take care to avoid games with small starting stacks, rapidly increasing levels (perhaps every 10 hands or so) and big jumps in blind increments.

You should also take note of any differences in structures between sites and key points in the structure that may require forward planning in your strategy. For example, consider the structure of a PokerStars turbo and a Full Tilt turbo up to the 1000/2000 level:

PokerStars (Turbo)

Starting Stack – 1500

Level (Minutes)	Blinds	Ante	Time Elapsed
1	10/20		0-5
2	15/30		5-10
3	25/50		10-15
4	50/100		15-20
5	75/150		20-25
6	100/200		25-30
7	100/200	25	30-35
8	200/400	25	35-40
9	300/600	50	40-45
10	400/800	50	45-50
11	600/1200	75	50-55
12	800/1600	75	55-60
13	1000/2000	100	60-65

Full Tilt Poker (Turbo)

Starting Stack – 1500

Level (Minutes)	Blinds	Ante	Time Elapsed
1	15/30		0-3
2	20/40		3-6
3	25/50		6-9
4	30/60		9-12
5	40/80		12-15
6	50/100		15-18
7	60/120		18-21
8	80/160		21-24
9	100/200		24-27
10	120/240		27-30
11	150/300		30-33
12	200/400		33-36
13	250/500		36-39
14	300/600		39-42
15	400/800		42-45
16	500/1000		45-48
17	600/1200		48-51
18	800/1600		51-54
19	1000/2000		54-57

Here although both games begin with 1500 chips per player and are likely to last a similar amount of time, there are some important differences that affect how they will play out in-between. For example, the starting stack on PokerStars is 75 big blinds whereas on Full Tilt it is 50 big blinds, and the blinds on PokerStars go up slower but more aggressively at certain points, whereas on Full Tilt the rises come rapidly but the increments are small. Also PokerStars introduces an ante after the 100/200 level, whereas Full Tilt does not have an ante at any point.

These are fairly obvious points that most players should be able to pick out, but it is important to think about how the structure is likely to affect you at key points in a sitngo, and when those points are likely to be reached. For example, as you approach the later stages these two structures diverge significantly, with the increments on Full Tilt being fairly smooth (100/200, 120/240, 150/300, 200/400) but those on PokerStars plateauing with the introduction of antes and then doubling sharply (100/200, 100/200/a25, 200/400/a25). Therefore you will need to plan ahead much more in the late stages of a PokerStars turbo to ensure that you are not taken by surprise by a sudden increase in blinds at the 200/400/a25 level.

Turbo vs. standard speed sitngos

In recent years 'turbo' sitngos with levels of 3-5 minutes have become far more popular than the original 'standard speed' ones with levels of 5-10 minutes. There are many reasons for this, for example recreational players may prefer games that finish in 30-45 minutes and not want to commit to playing an event for over an hour, and they may also prefer a faster structure if they think that it reduces the edge of better players and allows them to gamble more. On the other hand, professional players may prefer to multi-table large numbers of turbo events which require less attention compared to standard speed ones if they believe that this yields them a higher overall hourly rate.

However, this is not to say that new and existing players should not at least experiment with playing standard speed sitngos as well, both because of their profitability at a time when many sitngo pros simply ignore them and elect to register for every turbo event, and the advancements they will bring to your game since you will have to make more complex decisions. It should also be noted that standard speed sitngos will yield you a far higher ROI than turbos (and certainly be at least comparable in hourly rate terms) with far less variance, and less rake going to the sites who charge the same fee for both standard and turbo events, despite the latter lasting half as long.

How much should you expect to pay in entry fees?

Poker sites make profits from sitngos by charging an entry fee on top of the buy-in which varies according to the size of the event. At the lower stakes this will normally be around 10% of the buy-in, but as the stakes rise it will decrease to 5% at the higher levels. Therefore a reasonable set of buy-in levels and fees should look like the following, with a decreased entry fee percentage compensating for the increased skill level of your opponents and a decreasing edge as you move up in stakes:

Buy-in	Entry fee	Percentage ratio
$1000	+ $50 (and above)	5%
$500	+ $30	6%
$300	+ $20	6.66%
$200	+ $15	7.5%
$100	+ $9	9%
$50	+ $5 (and below)	10%

You should therefore avoid sites offering sitngos with fees significantly higher than these, as it will be extremely difficult to show any profit in the long term. You should also usually beware of 'jackpot' sitngos where a large prize can be collected for winning a number of consecutive games, since with this offer usually comes entry fees that are 50-100% higher than normal and are carefully calculated to at least offset the cost to the site of players claiming the jackpot.

A note on multi-tabling sitngos

Making money from poker is to a large extent a volume business (i.e. you must put in a lot of hands to expect a lot of profit), and in this respect turbo sitngos are ideal for players intent on grinding out a decent ROI over a large number of games in a short period through multi-tabling. If you are a beginning player you will be better off focusing on one or two games until you understand the fundamentals, but as your skill level and confidence increases so should the number of games you play.

How you approach multi-tabling should be a function of your own goals and capabilities, and is generally best determined through experience. As a guideline though, there are some players who manage to play more than 16 games at once with others feeling more comfortable with four or less. Predictably, the first group may therefore manage to play hundreds of games in a day with the latter coming nowhere close.

However, what is most important is finding your own optimal conditions based on number of screens and number of hours of play per day vs. your overall ROI and profit per day. For example, there is no point playing 16 games for 12 hours a day if it turns you into a losing player, and to many players it may be worth accepting a slightly lower overall profit if this is the result of playing significantly less hours or tables but with a higher ROI due to increased focus.

Multi-tablers also face the issue of how to best structure their sessions and whether they should play sitngos in sets (all starting at once) or with staggered starts. This again depends on personal preference, with playing in sets usually being most time efficient and staggered play usually maximising your ROI in each individual sitngo since you will face less complex bubble situations simultaneously and instead have a production line of games in progress, many of which will not require serious attention while you deal with those at crucial points. Note however that the higher the stakes you play, the fewer games there will be available, and so the option of starting several big buy-in games at once will usually not be present.

Chapter Two

Other Considerations

Besides pre-game strategies that you should use everytime you play, there are also a number of concepts that should be understood before playing sitngos. These include some basic poker ideas, as well as more complex aspects of sitngo strategy that should prove useful as you continue through the following chapters.

Introducing position

You will hear the word position frequently in any instructional poker material, and it is a key concept in all forms of the game. It refers to both your seating position relative to the button in a game, and to who gets to act last in a given hand based on this (so if only the blinds are left in a hand the big blind will 'have position' on the small blind). For the purposes of this book we will talk about hands you can play in certain positions and consider them as the following:

Early position	Between six and nine players left to act behind you

Mid-position	Four or five players left to act behind you
Late position	The button and cut-off seats
In the blinds	The small and big blinds, who act last preflop and first postflop

Note that once the number of players remaining is very small, positions are mainly referred to by their individual names. For example, in a six-handed game these would be (in the order they must act preflop): under-the-gun, hijack, cut-off, button, small blind and big blind.

Introducing hand ranges

Whenever you or your opponent is involved in a hand you should not be thinking specifically of the two cards each player may be holding at that particular moment in time, but the entire range of hands that they may possibly hold or that you are representing. Taking this approach has wide-reaching implications for any poker game (indeed poker in essence is the interaction of hand ranges and players' abilities to determine and make decisions based on them), but in sitngos where players are frequently all-in preflop what should mainly be considered is the way that different hands or hand ranges play against each other in such situations.

Therefore we will often be discussing hand ranges in terms of how profitable they are in certain all-in situations, or as percentages of the overall number of hands that can be dealt. For example in a certain situation it may be advisable to go all-in (or call an all-in) with the hand range 6-6+, A-10o+, A-9s+, which means all pairs sixes and above, all offsuit aces A-10 and above and all suited aces A-9 and above. This range can also be expressed as a percentage of all hands possible (in this case approximately 9%) where 0% would be no hands and 100% would be every hand from 3-2o to A-A.

Introducing EV

Throughout this book there will be references to EV (Expected Value). This usually refers to the mathematical expectation of a certain play, and can be expressed as +EV meaning a play with a positive expectation (i.e. a profitable one), –EV (a negative one) or EV neutral (one with neither positive or negative expectation), but we will also apply it in more detail to late game play with specific values or percentages attached to certain plays or stack sizes.

It is important to note that in sitngos, because you are paid based on the position in which you finish, your tournament chips do not have a linear real money value as they would in a cash game. For this reason, we must think purely in terms of $EV (the expectation of a play in terms of real money) rather than cEV (its expectation in terms of tournament chips). This is particularly important since some plays can show a profit in terms of tournament chips won, but a loss in terms of real money (i.e. they are +cEV but -$EV) and therefore should not be made.

In order to do this we must first have a method of calculating the worth of tournament chips in real money for any given situation so that different outcomes can be considered. We will therefore now look at ICM (the Independent Chip Model), which is considered the best way of doing this.

Introducing ICM (the Independent Chip Model)

It should be obvious to even a beginning player that the value of your chips in a sitngo is non-linear. That is, despite receiving a certain amount of chips at the start of a sitngo for your buy-in, because you are paid based on your finishing position and are unable to cash them in during the game, their real money value is going to change throughout the event depending on the number of players remaining, their relative stack sizes and the payout structure.

For example, consider a 10-player $100 sitngo with a standard 50%/30%/20% payout structure where each player starts with 1000 chips. Despite the initial conversion rate of 1 chip = 10 cents, by the end of the sitngo when the winning player has all 10,000 chips those chips have only secured him the $500 first prize, meaning the conversion rate has dropped to 1 chip = 5 cents. However, if a player has only 1 chip when four players remain and another player is eliminated in an all-in confrontation the conversion rate of his last chip in now fractionally more than 1 chip = $200 as he is guaranteed to finish in at least third place.

The most accurate way of calculating the real money value of tournament chips at points in a sitngo where it is less obvious than in these examples is known as ICM (the Independent Chip Model). ICM is a way of calculating the value of tournament chips in real money by considering the stacks of all players and the prize structure, and then calculating their relative chances of finishing in certain places and the total real money equity they would accrue by doing so. It is extremely complicated to work out by hand and most players use programs that do such calculations for them instantaneously (see next chapter), but here is one detailed example considering the following situation:

Player	Stack Size	Payout Structure	Tournament Equity ($EV)
A	4000	1st $500	?
B	3000	2nd $300	?
C	2000	3rd $200	?
D	1000	4th $0	?

Here each of the four remaining players has a different proportion of the chips in play (40%/30%/20%/10%) and there are three prizes available on a standard payout structure of 50%/30%/20%. From this we need to calculate the current real money value of their chips (not withstanding factors like the position of the blinds and the players' relative ability which are addressed in the chapter 'The limitations of ICM' on page 113). We can do this according to ICM by calculating each player's chances of finishing in each position and multiplying this by the payout for that place, then adding together those values to find out each player's overall $EV.

The probability that each player finishes first is easy to calculate since it correlates directly to the proportion of the chips in play they have. For example, the probability of Player A winning is 4000/10,000 which equates to 0.4 or 40%. Therefore we can begin to tabulate our results as follows:

Player	Stack Size	P (1st)	P (2nd)	P (3rd)	P (4th)
A	4000	40%	?	?	?
B	3000	30%	?	?	?
C	2000	20%	?	?	?
D	1000	10%	?	?	?

After this we must calculate the other finishing probabilities, which is where things become more complicated. If we consider Player A first of all, his chances of finishing second are the sum total of the situations in which one of the other players wins and he beats the remaining two players. There are three possible cases here and each can be tabulated by multiplying the chance of another player winning the sitngo by the chance that Player A will have of beating the remaining players, with the latter measured as the proportion of chips Player A has of those remaining three players after the winners' chips are removed.

So for example if Player B wins (which we know will happen 30% of the time), there are now 7000 chips remaining and Player A will have a 4000/7000 chance of beating the other two players. Calculating and adding all these values together will give us the total probability that Player A has of finishing second:

Outcome	Calculation	Probability
P (B wins and A beats C and D for 2nd)	0.3*(4000/7000)	= 0.1714

P (C wins and A beats B and D for 2nd)	0.2*(4000/8000)	= 0.1
P (D wins and A beats B and C for 2nd)	0.1*(4000/9000)	= 0.0444
P (All cases where A finishes 2nd)		**= 0.3158 (31.58%)**

Calculating the odds of Player A finishing third is even more complicated. We must consider the probability of another player winning outright, and multiply this by the chances that among the three remaining players another player wins this mini-tournament (to finish second overall) and then Player A beats the remaining player to finish third. There are six possible cases in which this can happen and they can be considered according to the exact finishing positions of the player from first to last. When tabulated this looks like:

Outcome	Calculation	Probability
P (finishing order of BCAD)	0.3*(2/7*4/5)	= 0.0686
P (finishing order of CBAD)	0.2*(3/8*4/5)	= 0.06
P (finishing order of BDAC)	0.3*(1/7*4/6)	= 0.0286
P (finishing order of DBAC)	0.1*(3/9*4/6)	= 0.0222
P (finishing order of CDAB)	0.2*(1/8*4/7)	= 0.143
P (finishing order of DCAB)	0.1*(2/9*4/7)	= 0.0127
P (All cases where A finishes 3rd)	**0.3*(2/7*4/5)**	**= 0.2064**

Having calculated the probability of A finishing first to third it is now easy to calculate his chances of finishing fourth since this is simply:

$$P \text{ (A finishes 4th)} = 1 - P \text{ (A finishes 1st-3rd)} = 0.0778 \text{ (7.78\%)}$$

This gives us a complete set of results for Player A and the same approach can be used for each player giving us the following results for all players and all positions:

Player	Stack Size	P (1st)	P (2nd)	P (3rd)	P (4th)
A	4000	40%	31.58%	20.64%	7.78%
B	3000	30%	30.83%	26.19%	12.98%
C	2000	20%	24.13%	31.75%	24.12%
D	1000	10%	13.45%	21.43%	55.12%

So, having calculated the probabilities for all finishing positions all we need to do now to get a real money value for each player's stack size is multiply their chance of finishing in a certain position by the payout for that position and add these values (note that fourth places can be excluded as it pays nothing). For Player A this would be as follows:

$$\$EV \text{ of Player A} = (0.4 * \$500) + (0.3158 * \$300) + (0.2064 * \$200) = \$336.02$$

And so the overall worth of each player's stack from the $1000 prize pool (allowing for rounding off) looks like this:

Player	Stack Size	Payout Structure	T'nmt Equity ($EV)
A	4000	1st $500	$336.03
B	3000	2nd $300	$294.87
C	2000	3rd $200	$235.89
D	1000	4th $0	$133.21

Harnessing the power of ICM

Performing calculations like this by hand takes a long time and is very impractical, but in the later stages of sitngos where the blinds are high and players usually move all-in with or fold most hands, understanding how your $EV is affected by such decisions is essential. For this reason most sitngo players use programs called ICM calculators, which not only calculate the $EV of your chips in any given situation but also determine whether certain all-in plays are profitable or not by considering the differences in your $EV between moving all-in and folding a given hand (and between calling and folding when another player has moved all-in), based on the situation and user-inputted hand ranges.

Of these, two products that are highly recommended are Sitngo Endgame Tools (www.sngegt.com) and Sitngo Wizard (www.sngwiz.com), both of which offer similar options to help work out whether you should move all-in ('push') or fold in certain situations according to ICM. Their relative merits are debatable, for example SNGEGT has a cleaner interface and a 'live play' version that you can use in real time[2], whereas Sitngo Wiz is capable of analysing more complex situations like multiple all-in scenarios. However, both offer free versions for you to decide which you prefer and so should be experimented with. At least one such program will be essential to your success as a sitngo player.

---

[2] Although some sites (such as PokerStars) have now banned this function. Please check with your site's terms and conditions if in doubt.

Chapter Three

The Early Game

Introducing the early game

The 'early game' in sitngos can be described as the period at the start of the sitngo where the average stack is fairly deep (e.g. 50-75 big blinds) and there is a full table of 9-10 players. It continues until the average stack is much lower and some players have been eliminated, altering the dynamic to one of short-handed, shorter-stacked play. We will look at the best approach based on a player's skill level, starting hand selection, games types and some of the possibilities for (and limitations to) deeper stack play, as well as discussing how best to maximise your edge without taking unnecessary risks. We will also consider tight vs. loose approaches and how your strategy should change as your stack size increases or decreases.

How well do you 'play poker'?

One of the key early game considerations for players new to sitngos should be the question 'How well do you 'play poker'?'. That is, how well do you make complex decisions about the play of hands based on a variety of factors such as your position, stack size, opponents, the betting that takes place, the texture of the flop and cards that follow, and so on. This is not intended to discourage new or inexperienced players – far from it in fact, as sitngos are the ideal training ground for these players.

The purpose of asking this question is to highlight that in sitngos it is not always necessary to 'play poker' in the early and middle stages where the blinds are small. This is because they will rise so rapidly and as they do you will be left with far simpler situations which will mainly revolve around decisions between moving all-in or folding, and calling or folding, which as we have seen can even be assisted by computer programs.

In fact, it may be most profitable for very inexperienced players to fold all but the strongest hands in the early game, and whatever your ability level your involvement at this stage should largely be based on your skill level in comparison to that of your opponents. So if you are a highly skilled player in comparison to the field you may want to enter quite a few more pots than if you are inferior to it. But if you have little or no poker experience at all you may just want to play extremely strong hands and otherwise wait for the blinds to rise to the point at which you can make straightforward all-in or fold decisions. In turbo sitngos at least, this point will be reached quite quickly so you will not sacrifice much of your stack in adopting such an approach.

Playable hands in the early game

Although you will want to play more or less hands during the early game depending on your overall ability level it is still important to understand in general which are playable and which are not. Therefore we will now look at these hands and some basic guidelines for how to play them, with the assumption that those not mentioned should be folded:

A-A

Of course, you should be looking to get as many chips in as possible preflop with pocket aces, whether by making a standard raise to 3-4 big blinds, reraising another player or limp-reraising from early position. Assuming that you end up in a raised pot against only a small number of opponents and are playing with stacks of 50-75 big blinds you should usually try to get the rest of your money in postflop unless the board is very scary.

K-K

The same applies with kings, although if an ace comes on the flop you will have to tread carefully and fold in situations where you face a lot of action or are against more than one player.

Q-Q

With queens you should be more careful about getting all-in against very tight or early position players preflop in higher stakes games (although you should rarely fold it elsewhere), but if you flop an overpair you should play in the same way as with aces or kings. You will face an overcard coming on the flop much more often however, and will need to play with caution in such circumstances.

J-J and 10-10

Although these are strong hands you should not usually look to get all-in with jacks or tens preflop for 50-75 big blinds (unless you are against very inexperienced or loose-aggressive players) and be more careful about reraising other players for this reason. You will also usually face at least one overcard on the flop with these hands, which is another reason to not reraise preflop and to play cautiously in raised pots after the flop. If you do flop an overpair you can still play your hand strongly, but you should beware of doing so in reraised pots where other players might have a higher pair, or when the board is very co-ordinated as even if you are ahead other players will often have draws with good equity because they contain overcards to your pair.

9-9 to 7-7

These hands should usually not be reraised preflop, although you may raise with them yourself since they will still have good equity postflop most of the time. They are however much more difficult to play than higher pairs if you do not flop a set, as there will usually be one or more overcards on the flop and so inexperienced players should tread carefully with them.

6-6 to 2-2

Small pairs are very difficult to play postflop without flopping a set and so should only be played in situations where you can expect to see the flop cheaply or open in late position. In tough games, or if you are inexperienced, folding them most of the time unless you can limp or call a raise in late position in a multiway pot would be advisable.

A-K

Although A-K is a very strong hand, as we will see later in this section you should not usually be looking to get an all-in with it preflop whilst the stacks are very deep for ICM reasons, unless you are facing weaker players who are willing to get all-in with A-Q or worse unpaired hands. You should, however, play it in most other situations and either raise or reraise and then usually be prepared to get the rest of your money in postflop if you hit top pair or better.

A-Q

Beware of playing A-Q too aggressively preflop against tight or early position players, and only reraise loose or late position players, and be prepared to get all-in against those who will do so with A-J or worse unpaired hands. Postflop, as with A-K, making top pair or better on a non-threatening board should usually be enough to put a lot of chips in.

A-J and A-10

These weaker broadway aces are still playable (especially if suited) but should be folded or played with caution against tight or early position players. Similarly you may want to fold them in early position in tough games or if you are inexperienced, and be more biased towards calling raises with them if you are going to play them than to reraise. Again, flopping top pair is a strong hand but be cautious in situations where you may be beaten by a better ace or overpair or if you pair your kicker but it is not top pair.

A9s-A2s

Suited 'rag' aces have slightly more value than unsuited ones, but not by much. You can open with them in late position like unsuited ones, and if there are many players in the pot you may also limp behind in late position in the hopes of flopping a flush draw or two pair.

A9o-A2o

These 'rag' aces should not be played unless you are opening on the cut-off or button, and even then you may want to fold them if you are up against tough opponents in the blinds or are inexperienced, as they will be difficult to play postflop even if you flop an ace.

Suited broadway (K-10s+, Q-10s+, J-10s)

These hands play well in both heads-up and multiway pots, as they can flop big draws as well as top pair with a good kicker, and so are playable in many situations. However you should proceed with caution when you have made only one pair and are facing a lot of action, and you may not want to play them in early position in tough games or if you are inexperienced.

Unsuited broadway (K-10o+, Q-10o+, J-10o)

These hands lose considerable value from not being suited as you will mainly make one-pair hands that you cannot play with total confidence as you may be dominated. However they can still be opened in late position and played with some confidence when you flop top pair.

Lower suited connectors

Hands like 9-8s or 7-6s are playable in select spots in sitngo such as when you can limp in late position behind other players, or your table is loose-passive, but you should not usually be raising with them yourself unless opening in late position and only call raises in multiway pots where you have a skill advantage over your opponents.

What type of game are you in?

An additional factor to consider when selecting starting hands in the early game is the type of game you are in, which can be categorised into four main groups:

Tight-aggressive

Few players see each flop and there is usually at lease one raise preflop.

Tight-passive

Few players see each flop but there is rarely a raise preflop.

Loose-aggressive

Many players see each flop and there is usually at least one raise preflop.

Loose-passive

Many players see each flop and there is rarely a raise preflop.

Your goal at the start of a sitngo should be to begin working out which label most fits the game you are in. This might be made easier if you have played with some of the players before, if you have looked up their results, or if you are playing higher stakes (where games will tend towards being tight-aggressive). Irrespective of this however, you should be able to develop a feel for it in the first few minutes based on how many raises and calls there are preflop in each hand. You should then adjust your strategies as follows:

Tight-aggressive games

There will be little value in limping speculative hands like small pairs and suited connectors in early position as players will raise to isolate you and not many players will see each flop, denying you the odds to call these raises. Therefore you should play tight as well and open hands you play for a raise, but beware of players reraising you as they will frequently have a strong hand.

Tight-passive games

Again there will be little value in limping speculative hands in early position as there will rarely be enough callers to make doing so worthwhile, although the decreased likelihood of isolation raises should make it slightly more attractive. Be particularly wary of players entering the pot, whether they call or raise, as they could have very strong hands and you should avoid giving them a lot of action with marginal hands.

Loose-aggressive games

There will be value here in playing your big hands deceptively (e.g. limp-reraising high pairs and A-K in early position) and hoping to trap people, or playing strong multiway hands in late position even for a raise. Beware, however, of getting too involved with speculative hands and draws which could prove expensive and play a relatively tight-passive game unless you have a strong hand yourself.

Loose-passive

These games are ideal for making speculative limps even in

early position with hands like small pairs and suited connectors as you will hope to see many cheap multiway flops and not pay too much to chase your draws. Beware of trying to bully players and buy pots in such games, however, as this strategy could prove costly.

Limping vs. raising

Any time you are first to enter the pot you will have the option of folding, calling or raising. Assuming you find a hand you consider playable, however, you should only be open-limping in early position, or in late position if other players have limped in front of you. This is because the closer you are to the button and the blinds the more valuable it is to you to try and force the other players out with a raise to gain position and try to pick up the blinds uncontested, particularly as they increase in size.

Limping in mid- or late position when other players have already limped is acceptable, however, as you will already be getting inviting pot odds as well as the security of good position and the reduced likelihood of anyone raising behind you. In fact, with a marginal hand in mid- or late position you should be more inclined to limp after other players than raise than you would in a cash game or tournament in order to avoid creating large pots where you are only a marginal favourite.

Assuming that you play better than the majority of your opponents and have a favourable table for limping in early position (i.e. one that is predominately loose-passive), you may want to limp with small to medium pairs and even good suited connectors, as well as some hands that you might otherwise raise in order to balance your overall limping range. You will also want to limp in early position sometimes in a loose-aggressive game, but here it will be with the intention of reraising with your strongest hands (Q-Q+ and A-K). Note that suited connectors, small pairs and medium strength aces are difficult hands to play profitably in early position in a tight or loose-aggressive game and that consequently you should usually fold them.

Once one or more players have limped in front of you most of the hands mentioned above will be playable in mid-late position, although in marginal situations you should also consider the type of game you are in and your skill level. In very favourable situations, like on the button when several mediocre players have limped or on the small blind after limpers you may also want to call with gap-connectors (e.g. 9-7s), any Broadway hand and suited rag aces, as you will be getting excellent pot odds.

Except in these situations you should usually enter the pot with a raise of 3-4 big blinds if you intend to play a hand – that is anytime you have five or fewer players behind you, unless you are in an exceptional situation like being the small blind when everyone else has folded. Most of the hands above can be raised from late position, and you should also usually be raising in early position with very strong hands that you wish to play (unless you have a reason to trap) and after limpers, where you should add on approximately one big blind to your raise for each limper.

Playing in the blinds

Playing in the blinds in the early stages of a sitngo is more complex as you will already have money committed and will be offered either a free or discounted look at a flop. However, because of your bad position and the shallow stack sizes you should still not play many hands, only completing the small blind with hands that figure to have good implied odds as already discussed and only calling a raise from the big blind with good aces, small pairs and high suited connectors (of course you would still reraise most of the time with premium hands), as otherwise you may flop a marginal hand that will be hard to play profitably out of position.

One special situation to take note of in the early game is playing the small blind when everyone else has folded around to you. Again, in this spot you should not play hands indiscriminately, but it is worth limping with a few more hands than you would in other situations as you are getting 3-1 pot odds if the big blind does not raise. In addition, you will also be able to get a sense of his reaction to limping whilst it is still cheap to do. This will help you in the later stages of the sitngo where with large blinds you might decide to limp again with a very big hand to trap an aggressive player, or with a mediocre one against a passive player whom you believe will let you see a cheap flop where you might be able to outplay them.

Calling raises, reraising and moving all-in

The early stages of sitngo play are usually much tighter than in other forms of no-limit hold'em because of factors like inexperienced players waiting for the blinds to rise and multi-tablers who have too many games running to play a lot of speculative hands (although this might not be true of very low buy-in games). You should therefore be much more careful with reraising and moving all-in after a player has reraised you and often just opt to call raises from tight players even with stronger hands.

This is because taking close gambles in large pots is generally a bad idea since (as ICM shows us) the more chips you have the less they are worth individually[3], and also because losing a significant percentage of your stack in a marginal situation can cause problems for you later in a sitngo. Therefore when a very tight player opens in early position you should consider just calling with (or even throwing away) hands as big as A-Qo and just calling with pairs as big as J-J.

Similarly, when a very tight player raises in mid- position you should still be cautious about reraising with hands like A-J or A-10 which could be dominated (although A-Q and A-K are now reraise worthy), and medium pairs like 8-8, 9-9 and 10-10 (although reraising with J-J+ is now fine) as you may be re-reraised all-in and forced to fold, and even if you get to the flop these hands will often face overcards and you will be left with awkward decisions in situations where you may have to play for your entire stack.

Against loose-aggressive players your ranges should be wider than these, but you should still be inclined to add more hands to your range for calling raises than to your reraising range since these players will often be looking to gamble and will move all-in with a wide range. By doing this you will avoid expensive situations like getting reraised all-in and having to either call all-in in a marginal situation or fold and forgo your chips as well as the chance of seeing a cheap flop.

When you do reraise and your opponent moves all-in you will have to make an assessment of his particular range of hands for doing this and act accordingly. However, most solid players will not make this move in the

---

[3] A concept originally outlined in *Gambling Theory and Other Topics* by Mason Malmuth.

early game without a very tight range along the lines of A-K, J-J+, and despite the chips you have put in the pot already because of your aversion to gambling in large pots you should probably still only be calling with a range like Q-Q+ (and not even Q-Q if J-J is below his pushing range), unless you are facing an inexperienced or loose-aggressive player.

Similarly, if you are reraised by a solid player then A-K, Q-Q+ is probably a sensible range to move all-in with. If you have opened in late position or been reraised by a very loose-aggressive player then adding 10-10, J-J and A-Q is reasonable too. We will now consider some of these situations in more detail using ICM.

ICM considerations for early game play

We can use ICM to explain these strategies further through analysis of your $EV in certain situations, which demonstrates why getting all-in with even strong hands during the early game can be problematic. To do this consider how a hand like A-K should be played which, although powerful, can still be -$EV if you end up all-in against a tight player whilst the stacks are still deep.

We have already seen that good players will have very tight reraising and all-in ranges in sitngos. Despite this A-K will still fair well against all but the tightest, for example if suited it is a 52.53% favourite against the range J-J+, A-Q+. However whilst this edge would be enough justification to play it in a cash game, if someone moved all-in before you with that range in a sitngo you must consider how your $EV changes based on the worth of your new chip stack if you win or lose.

To do this consider a 10-player $100 sitngo, with a total of $1000 prize money to be paid out on a standard 50%/30%/20% structure. At the start of the event the distribution of equity (ignoring any entry fee or blinds) will be:

Player	Stack Size	Tournament Equity ($EV)
1	1500	$100
2	1500	$100

3	1500	$100
4	1500	$100
5	1500	$100
6	1500	$100
7	1500	$100
8	1500	$100
9	1500	$100
10	1500	$100

Now consider the scenario where Players 9 and 10 go all-in on the first hand in a 'coin-flip' situation. One will be eliminated, and the other will double up to 3000 chips. However, because of the effect of the payout structure and the fact that there is now one less player to be eliminated before the money is reached, the winning player's stack is not worth double its original value according to ICM, and the bystanders in this hand have gained equity from the confrontation, making the new situation:

Player	Stack Size	Tournament Equity ($EV)
1	1500	$101.94
2	1500	$101.94
3	1500	$101.94
4	1500	$101.94
5	1500	$101.94
6	1500	$101.94
7	1500	$101.94
8	1500	$101.94
9	3000	$184.48

So, despite having won chips on the hand, Player 9 was in fact in a -$EV situation overall. Half the time his $EV will go from $100 to $0, and half the time from $100 to $184.48, meaning his overall loss on the hand is:

$$($184.48/2) - $100 = -$7.76$$

Again, discounting the effect of the entry fee and the blinds, we can then calculate the minimum percentage favourite Player 9 would need to be in that hand to show a profit as:

$$x\% = ($100/$184.48)*100 = 54.21\%$$

Therefore, if a player moves all-in on the first hand of a sitngo, you should fold A-Ks even if you know he has the range J-J+, A-Q+ against which you are a 52.53% favourite as you stand to lose overall in $EV terms. This will also still be the case if a player moves all-in over the top of your opening raise with this range, since the pot odds you are getting will not be that compelling compared to your overall loss of equity.

If you reraise someone however and are put all-in by an aggressive player with this range you will now be in a closer situation. Here the pot odds do start to have significance as you may have put as much as 15-20% of your stack in already. For example if you reraised to 200 and folded your remaining 1300 chips would be worth $87.72 and if you reraised to 300 and folded your remaining chips would be worth $81.48. As we have seen, when you call and win your $EV is $184.48, meaning that to break even in $EV terms in the first instance you would need to win 47.55% of the time and 44.17% in the second.

However, in such a situation your opponent's range will generally be much tighter than that outlined above and for this reason you should probably still fold against a good player. For example, against a range of Q-Q+, A-K you will only win 41.9% of the time (and adding J-J does not change this significantly), so even with 20% of your stack in the middle you would still need to fold here unless you believe your opponents range includes A-Q, which would tip things in your favour.

How your strategy changes as your chip stack increases

We have just seen that as your chip stack increases in a sitngo so too the worth of each individual chip decreases, to the point at which you have all the chips but only 50% of the total prize pool. For this reason, as your stack increases in the early stages of a sitngo you should be more inclined to play aggressively with these additional chips when you have hands like big draws in order to start building up a stack that can dominate on the bubble, where the full power of your chip lead can be unleashed.

There are two reasons for this. Firstly, the more chips you have, the closer the percentage favourite you will need to be in an all-in situation to break even in $EV terms returns to 50%, making you more indifferent to ICM constraints as your opponents become more influenced by them. Secondly, by playing more aggressively in marginal situations such as with strong drawing hands you will be able to apply pressure to opponents who must risk elimination if they lose, and thus pick up chips when they are forced to fold.

How your strategy changes if your chip stack decreases

When your chip stack decreases in the early stages of a sitngo, the reverse of the above applies as your remaining chips will be more valuable individually than those you have lost, in accordance with the principles we have already discussed. For example, if you lose half your stack immediately the remaining chips are worth quite a bit more than half your initial buy-in:

(see following table)

Because of this, you should not panic if you lose a big pot early on as your stack will be more valuable than it appears, and if the blinds are still small you will have to plenty of time to regain chips. Similarly, as the blinds increase you will be the first player able to move all-in with a short stack which will provide you with valuable leverage against other stacks, assuming that you are not extremely short. Depending on the size of your remaining stack in big blinds you should adopt the strategies recommended in later sections of this book for playing with shorter stack sizes.

Player	Stack Size	Tournament Equity ($EV)
1	1500	$100.48
2	1500	$100.48
3	1500	$100.48
4	1500	$100.48
5	1500	$100.48
6	1500	$100.48
7	1500	$100.48
8	1500	$100.48
9	2250	$143.75
10	750	$52.41

Thoughts on tight vs. loose play in the early game

There are generally two schools of thought regarding playing the early stages of a sitngo. On the one side are players that advocate playing extremely tight in order to preserve your stack for the later stages where any additional chips will add leverage to your all-in moves and make it more difficult for other players to call you (this is also the strategy of high-volume multi-tablers, although their reasons are more to do with practicality).

On the other side are those who advocate a looser approach and speculating with a portion of your chips in the early stages (perhaps as much as 20-30%) in the hopes of making a big hand and doubling through early, thereby massively increasing your prospects for the sitngo as a whole.

As we have already seen, both of these approaches are acceptable in the right circumstances and should be utilised by players according to their skill levels and the type of game in which they are playing. It is, however, worth remembering that many players overestimate their ability to play certain hands in certain positions profitably, and that you should not take playing speculative hands early to an extreme.

Nor should you be prepared to speculate away too large a proportion of your stack early, and if you do lose a significant percentage then tightening up and waiting for the blinds to rise and meet your stack at a level where you will have increased leverage is probably advisable unless you find a good opportunity. For example, if you get down to 900 chips at the 25-50 level in a PokerStars sitngo you would be well advised to play extremely tight and preserve as many chips as possible for the 50-100 level where you can begin moving your stack all-in to either increase it significantly by winning the blinds.

Postflop play in the early stages of sitngos

When you get to a flop the pot will either be heads-up or multiway, and either you will have the initiative from being the preflop raiser, someone else will, or no-one will if it is a limped pot. You will also be in position or out of position (or perhaps somewhere in the middle in a multiway pot), which will be key in determining the extent to which you can control the hand.

Generally on the flop you should bet around 2/3 to 3/4 of the pot as a continuation bet when you are heads-up and have the initiative whether you make a hand or not, unless your opponent is very loose, the board is very draw heavy or you have flopped a monster and think trapping is the best play. When someone else has the initiative in a heads-up pot, you should generally check to them and then play accordingly. In multiway pots with the initiative, you should continuation bet far less with no hand, although betting dry flops like K♣-7♠-2♥ against two tight players is usually profitable.

On the turn and river you will need to reassess according to the cards that have come and how they affect your hand, the number of players remaining, the amount of chips left and your position. Thinking about the size of pot you wish to play is always key and for this reason position is crucial and you should think early in a hand about whether you are prepared to commit all your chips with it.

Your bet sizing (and that of other players) will also be crucial on these later streets as you will often be all-in if you bet both the turn and river. For this reason you should plan ahead when choosing amounts according to the number of big blinds you have left, although betting 2/3-3/4 of the pot is still a good general guideline. As a general rule, in limped pots you should not usually put all your money in unless you have two pair or better, and you should try to build or restrict the size of the pot accordingly.

As previously stated, very inexperienced players should not play many hands in the early stages of sitngos, particularly if they do not feel comfortable with postflop decisions. However, there are still several categories of hands for which the appropriate strategy is fairly clear and we will look at these now:

Monster hands

These are extremely strong hands that are virtually guaranteed to win the pot like flopped sets, straights, flushes or full houses. How you should play them depends on how draw heavy the flop is, and the more scare cards there are that could come on the turn and river the more chips you should look to get into the pot on the flop. In the case of a flopped full house for example, you are virtually invulnerable and may want to slowplay, especially if there are draws on the flop that may allow your opponent to make a flush or straight on a later street, but with 6♥-6♣ on a 6♠-7♠-9♥ flop you should be betting and raising to get all-in as early as possible.

Top pair, good kicker or overpair to the board

Here you will usually want to bet aggressively for value and to protect your hand, and get as much money in as possible against aggressive and loose opponents. Against tight ones, on very draw heavy boards (such as 7♥-8♥-9♣ or K♠-10♠-J♠) or in multiway pots you should proceed more cautiously and even consider folding to a lot of action from multiple opponents unless your hand also has drawing potential (such as 10♣-10♥ on a 7♥-8♥-9♣ flop, or A♠-K♦ on a K♠-10♠-J♠ flop, which are monster hands).

Strong draws

With reasonably strong draws that have around 12 outs you should be wary of putting too much action in as you will rarely be better than a coin-flip, and as we have seen coin-flips are usually -$EV in the early stages of sitngos. However, when you have a very strong draw with 15 or more outs such as A♠-Q♠ on a J♠-10♠-5♥ board or 7♥-8♥ on a 5♥-6♥-J♣ board you are likely to be a favourite against most hands and should be more inclined to put in a lot of action and even get all-in. Even if called by a very strong hand you will still have significant equity, plus you will sometimes win the pot uncontested and opponents will not be able to always put you on strong made hands in the future.

Weaker draws

Draws with 8-12 outs are still playable in the early game but should be played cautiously and in small pots where you have good implied odds when you hit. For example, two way straight draws like 9♣-8♣ on an A♠-6♦-7♣ board or flush draws like 7♣-6♣ on an A♣-5♣-10♠ board are worth pursuing for small amounts in small (or multiway) pots where you are getting good odds on the flop, but not expensively on the turn or without good odds. Draws where some of your outs could be tainted (i.e. you could make them and still lose to a better hand) or you could already be drawing dead like 7♠-8♠ on a 5♥-6♥-K♥ board or 8♥-9♥ on a K♠-10♥-K♥ board should be folded or pursued with extreme caution, and very weak draws like gutshots with four outs or less should not be pursued at all.

Combination draws

When you have a pair and a draw you generally have a powerful hand, however as with other draws in sitngos you still need to be circumspect unless it is very strong. For example, 9♥-8♥ on an 9♠-5♥-6♥ board is an extremely strong combo draw that you would be happy to go all-in with on the flop, whereas 6♠-5♣ on a 4♦-5♣-8♥ board is far weaker, meaning that you could easily be dominated and should therefore play it slowly or even fold it to a strong bet.

Weak one-pair hands

These hands are very situational and require you to 'play poker' in determining the best course of action. For example, having raised in late position with A♠-J♣ and been called by one blind to see a flop of K♠-J♦-4♥ is very different to being in the big blind in a limped pot with Q♥-3♠ and seeing a flop of Q♦-10♦-7♥ along with three other players. Generally speaking the best course of action in such spots is to try and show the hand down cheaply, and fold if it seems likely that a big pot is likely to ensue or many players remain in it.

No hand

Having no hand on the flop is not that much of a disaster if you have the initiative in a heads-up pot, as you will still often win with a continuation bet. In other situations, however, you should just be prepared to give up and save your chips for a better situation since elaborate bluffs are overrated in poker in general and in sitngos in particular.

Chapter Four

The Middle Game

Introducing the middle game

The middle game is the period where the blinds have risen significantly so that the average stack size limits deep-stacked strategies, and you now are playing a more short-handed game than initially, but not quite at the bubble or required to play all-in or fold poker yet. We will see how strategies change at this stage due to playing with shorter and more diverse stack sizes and fewer players, and how players must now tighten up significantly, whilst still being able to make normal sizes raises and to make continuation bets on the flop. We will also look at how your preflop hand selection should alter as your stack diminishes in relation to the growing blinds, and how the decreasing number of players affects your decisions in terms of playing all-in pots according to ICM considerations.

Introducing effective stack sizes

At this stage of the sitngo players will usually have varied stack sizes, and when you are playing a hand you will need to think in terms of effective stack sizes, i.e. the maximum amount of chips that can be won or lost in a given hand between certain players. For example, if the blinds are

50/100 and you open on the button to 300 with 2400 chips in total with the remaining players having 1200 and 4200, the effective stack sizes would be different if each of them moved all-in. Against the small blind you would be playing for all their chips but not all of your own, so the effective stack size would be 1200, but if the big blind moved all-in you would be playing for all your chips but not all of his, so the effective stack size would be 2400.

Any time you play a pot in the mid-late stages of a sitngo it is very important that you consider the stack sizes of players who have entered the pot before you and those that remain behind in terms of big blinds, how you will want to play against them with your hand based on this, and whether you will have chips remaining if you lose an all-in. Forward thinking in this manner can save you from getting trapped into calling a reraise with a marginal hand, not having the right sized stacks to continuation bet, or otherwise putting yourself in a position where the stack sizes are awkward.

How preflop hand selection alters as your stack size diminishes

As your stack size in terms of big blinds diminishes, you should tend to play fewer speculative hands and limp less (and when it is very low not at all). With a moderate sized stack of 30-50 big blinds there will still be some play in the game and most of the hands mentioned in the section on the early game will still be playable, but you should usually be opening the pot with raises in order to give yourself the chance to gain additional chips immediately or with a continuation bet, and generally aim to play a streamlined version of early game strategy.

As your stack size drops further your options will become more limited and with 15-30 big blinds, whilst you are still able to make normal sized raises and continuation bet in favourable situations, you should tighten your opening ranges significantly both because you have fewer chips behind if things go wrong and because other players will have ideal sized stacks for reraising all-in with. At this point in particular then it is important that you know how your opponents play and whether they are likely to play back at you, so that you can identify situations where it might be better to fold or to raise with a marginal hand.

A note on blind stealing in sitngos

In the middle game you will see the blinds rise and the average size of your stack (in terms of big blinds) diminish rapidly. Therefore you will need to give some thought to how best to maintain it and to gain additional chips as you move towards the bubble stages and face the prospect of extreme blind pressure. However, for a number of reasons you should not attempt to solve this problem by making frequent attempts to steal the blinds (i.e. raise with a bad hand because of your position), unless you expect to succeed in this a very high proportion of the time.

Firstly, unlike in multi-table tournaments where the middle game will be extremely long and the blind increases gradual, which makes a stack that can keep out of trouble by stealing desirable, in a sitngo the middle game will be extremely short and you will usually be unable to maintain a stack that allows you to keep stealing because of the rapidly rising blinds. This means that unless stealing is going to be profitable in itself it is of little use, and this will rarely be the case because during the middle game so many players will have ideal sized stacks to reraise you all-in. They will also do so with even wider ranges if they believe that you are stealing too often, since you will usually have to fold for ICM reasons.

Similarly, losing a portion of your chips on a steal if you have to raise and continuation bet or fold to a reraise will reduce your options later on in the sitngo, as well as reducing your $EV by significantly more than winning the same amount of chips would increase it by. You will also find yourself getting all-in in some more marginal postflop situations, which could be disastrous for your $EV. Therefore in the middle game you should mainly open with stronger hands or reraise other players in order to maintain your stack, and preserve the rest of your chips for the late game and beyond when you can move all-in or fold.

A note on the size of your opening raise as the blinds increase

As the blinds increase, and the average stack in terms of big blinds decreases, you should not be opening for more than three big blinds and you may also want to consider lowering the size of your raise to 2.5 big blinds as the average stack drops to 15-20 big blinds. This will be more economical and usually have the same effect as a larger raise since players are under more pressure in the middle game, and you will also be less committed to call a reraise if there are players behind you with 10-15 big blind stacks than if you make a standard raise.

Additionally, opening to 2.5 big blinds will bring down the size of the continuation bets that you will need to make, which can be very useful when you are dealing with very shallow stack sizes or wish to preserve chips yourself with a stack of 15-20 big blinds. With a stack of exactly 15 big blinds, for example, opening for 2.5 big blinds will still leave you 12.5 behind and if you get called in one position (making the pot 5.5-6.5 big blinds, depending on whether it is one of the blinds) you will still be able to afford to continuation bet for 3-4 big blinds and fold to a reraise if you have no hand.

Reraising and flat calling a raise in the middle game

As the average stack size by big blinds drops, you will need to start planning your bet sizing more precisely, particularly in reraised pots. For example, with around 50 big blinds you will still be able to play a fairly standard game, however by the time your stack is below 30 big blinds you will no longer be able to reraise an opponent and continuation bet comfortably on the flop without committing yourself to a hand.

With a stack of over 30 big blinds you will have the option of smooth calling a raise or reraising a standard amount to around nine big blinds (assuming an opening raise of three big blinds) and playing from there. In multi-table tournaments you will be able to make steal reraises to around nine big blinds in such situations against loose-aggressive players in an attempt to accumulate chips. However, in sitngos, where players tend to open more tightly and you want to avoid risking your stack in marginal situations, this strategy tends to be sub-optimal and so your reraises should mainly be for value.

With a stack of 20-30 big blinds however, since you cannot reraise without committing yourself to a hand you should usually just reraise all-in yourself or flat call. This is because the former will give you the benefit of considerable fold equity against an opponent for ICM reasons, and the latter will avoid large confrontations with hands that you want to play but don't feel are strong enough to raise all-in with, and also allow you to occasionally smooth-call with very big hands to trap your opponent or give an aggressive player behind you the opportunity to 'squeeze'. That said, you should not be playing many hands in either of these ways because of the stack sizes. For example, even with a stack of 20 big blinds reraising a three big blind opener is risking a lot to win a little (20 big blinds to win 4.5), and with relatively shallow stack sizes smooth-calling with a lot of marginal hands will not be profitable.

For these reasons, with deeper stacks of 20-30 big blinds you should generally only be reraising players all-in when your hand figures to be significantly ahead of their range but is not necessarily comfortable seeing a flop (e.g. A-K, Q-Q, J-J and 10-10 against early position players and slightly worse against late position players). However if your hand only figures to be slightly ahead of their range (e.g. A-Q, A-J or against tight or early position players) or is a genuine monster than has postflop potential (i.e. A-A or K-K) with these stack sizes you may be better off smooth-calling rather than escalating the action.

With a stack of 15-20 big blinds, however, you are in an ideal position for reraising other players all-in as it will afford you significant fold equity without risking unnecessary chips. You should still remember though that you do not want to get in unnecessary all-in situations as the bubble approaches, and so frequently making plays like re-stealing all-in or reraising all-in with marginal hands against loose players who are apt to call with a wide range will not usually be profitable.

Instead you should focus on looking for situations where either your hand is extremely strong and does not mind being called, or your opponent is unlikely to call (either because of his position or opening range) and you have something with reasonable equity if you happen to be called. Bear in mind, however, that in cases where the effective stacks are 15-20 big blinds but you have significantly more chips than your opponent, that you can now play slightly looser, as losing some of your chips will not be as big a disaster in ICM terms and the fold equity you have in the sitngo format is considerable.

Being reraised

When you have opened a pot and been reraised, you should not be playing many hands, even if you suspect that your opponent is likely to make occasional loose reraises. When you are playing with deeper stacks you will usually either have been moved all-in on or reraised about three times your opening raise. If a player has moved all-in on you for 20-30 big blinds this is usually a very strong hand and you should not be calling with many hands at all because you will only be getting pot odds of around 3-2 and this will not compensate for the damage done to your $EV when you are behind. In fact, if a tight player raises you all-in in this scenario and you will be all-in you might fold hands as strong as 10-10 or A-Q.

If you are playing with deeper stacks and you are reraised around three times your opening raise you will need to take a view of that player's hand range and act accordingly. For example, you will need to assess whether your opponent is likely to make such a raise as a re-steal or if it is more likely to be a monster hand looking for action. Since such a raise tends to put an opponent in an awkward position if he has close to 30 big blinds, you may even consider calling and taking a flop with a very big hand if you are not sure he is committed to calling a reraise all-in, or if you have a marginal hand against his range but are likely to gain equity by seeing a flop if he is likely to push all-in even if he has missed.

Against shallower stacks of 15-20 big blinds you will need to consider a variety of factors when reraised, principally your opponents hand range, the pot odds that your are being offered, and whether you will have any chips remaining when you call. With effective stacks of 15 big blinds if you open for three big blinds and are reraised by a non-blind player you will be calling 12 big blinds to win 19.5 and with 20 big blinds 17 to win 24.5. Because these odds are not compelling you should still not be calling with a wide range of hands, although A-Q, A-J and medium pairs are now also reasonable in many situations, particularly when you have chips behind.

ICM considerations for middle game play

We can also quantify the percentage of the time you will need to win to break even in $EV terms in a given situation during the middle game using ICM. For example consider a game where there are now six players remaining with equal stack sizes:

Player	Stack Size	Tournament Equity ($EV)
Player 1 (BB)	2500	$166.67
Player 2 (SB)	2500	$166.67
Player 3 (Button)	2500	$166.67
Player 4	2500	$166.67
Player 5	2500	$166.66
Player 6	2500	$166.66

Now let's assume that Player 3 opens to 300 with blinds of 50/100 and that Player 1 reraises all-in. If Player 3 folds his new $EV will be $149.97 and if he calls and wins it will be only be $288.51 even though he is calling 2200 to win a pot of 5050. Therefore he will need still need to win at least 51.98% of the time against the all-in player's range even having committed over 10% of his stack. If the blinds were 75/150 and the opening raise was to 450 he would now be calling 2050 to win a pot of 5075 with his $EV standing at $141.39 if he folded and $289.43 if he called and won. Only at this point would he be able to call with less than 50% equity with the minimum win percentage now dropping to 48.85%. Therefore during the middle game it is important to remember that pot odds can often be less appealing than they might seem for ICM reasons.

Defending the blinds

With a stack size of 30-50 big blinds you should not be defending many hands from the blinds (especially the small blind where you have worse odds and are not closing the action). However, once the average stack falls below this size, and ideally with effective stacks of 15-20 big blinds, you will be able to start defending with a few more hands, either by reraising all-in preflop and putting your opponent to the test, or by calling from the big blind with hands that can flop well with the intention of checkraising all-in on favourable flops.

We have already seen that you should not be reraising all-in with many weak or semi-bluffing hands unless the conditions are optimal (i.e. you have chips behind and believe that your opponent is unlikely to call often). However, with effective stacks of 15-20 big blinds you may certainly reraise A-10+ and all pairs against late position raisers and looser mid-position raisers, as well as a few more hands depending on the exact situation.

However, because being all-in in marginal situations is very detrimental to your overall $EV, there will be some situations in which you should prefer to call a preflop raise in the big blind and opt to try and checkraise a continuation bet all-in on a favourable flop. This is generally a good strategy when you are not sure that reraising all-in is a +$EV play but you have a hand that is playable and can flop well (e.g. A-9s or K-Jo), you have a stack size that is ideal for checkraising all-in with (again 15-20 big blinds), and your opponent is likely to continuation bet.

This stack size is ideal because not only does it allow your opponent the option of continuation betting without committing to the hand (making him more likely to do so and giving you fold equity when you checkraise all-in with a draw), but it is also the correct size for you to happily put your money in when you do make a top pair type hand in the knowledge that the chips you win when it is good will far outweigh those that you lose when it is dominated.

Chapter Five

The Late Game

Introducing the late game

The late game is the stage in the sitngo when the blinds are too high to raise and continuation bet, and you must revert to an all-in or fold strategy. Sometimes you will get to the bubble, or even beyond it, whilst the blinds are still low, but often you will need to change your strategy to one of all-in or fold whilst there are still five or more players remaining. We will look at why moving all-in or folding becomes an optimal strategy at this stage and how to adapt to players who deviate from it, as well as how ICM affects your decisions as you approach the bubble.

The all-in zone

So far we have only discussed situations where your stack is deep enough that you are able to raise to around three big blinds and then make a continuation bet on the flop without committing yourself to a hand. However, once you drop below 15 big blinds it becomes difficult to do this, since raising and either checking the flop or committing most of your chips offers your opponent the chance to call your raise with the prospect of winning your whole stack if you bluff or being able to bluff you if you show no further interest in the pot. Similarly, because your stack is so short, limping should not be an option either in most situations.

By process of elimination therefore we can see that with this stack size your best option is to raise all-in and force your opponents to play for all your chips (or theirs) or fold preflop. This is particularly true in sitngos because most players will not call an all-in raise without a very strong hand for ICM reasons and prefer to wait for situations where they can move all-in themselves and win the blinds uncontested. Broadly speaking the all-in zone can be divided into three areas:

10-15 big blinds

This stack size is a no-man's land between the ideal stack for pushing all-in and the point at which you can comfortably afford to make a normal-sized raise and continuation bet without committing yourself to a hand. It is an awkward situation to be in, and you should generally play few hands and move all-in when you do. Note, however, that these will mostly need to be of a high quality (or you will need to have excellent position) as you will be risking a lot to win a little, and will have little or no fold-equity against a player that has raised before you.

5-10 big blinds

This is the ideal sized stack with which to move all-in, since it is large enough to put your opponents under pressure and deny them good pot odds to call with mediocre hands, but does not risk many chips, meaning that you can move all-in with a wide range in many situations. Most late stage sitngo play takes place with these stack sizes, and you should make every effort to ensure that you keep a stack of at least five big blinds as the blinds escalate in order to maintain your fold equity and allow you to pick up chips without showdowns most of the time.

0-5 big blinds

This stack size is usually reached when you have been unsuccessful in maintaining one of 5-10 big blinds or have recently lost an all-in and been left short-stacked. Not only are you in the position of having little or no fold equity when you push all-in, meaning that you will therefore need to find a good hand or a player under considerable chip pressure themselves to attack in the big blind, but going through the blinds yourself will cost 30% or more of your remaining chips. Once here you must simply look for the best situation to move your remaining chips all-in based on your hand, your stack size, the player in the big blind, the other stacks at the table, and how many hands you have before the big blind will hit you.

Playable hands in the late game

When deciding whether a hand is playable or not in the late game, your main considerations should be its value and your stack size in terms of big blinds, whether anyone has moved all-in already or you can move all-in first, and how many players are still to act behind you (or remaining in total). You should also consider the effective stack sizes, i.e. whether you cover a player who has already moved all-in (in which case you should usually reraise all-in or fold) or not, and whether or not you cover players who might call behind you if you move all-in.

Trying to determine exactly when a hand is playable is difficult if you are an inexperienced player, and for this reason you should use an ICM calculator like Sitngo Endgame Tools or Sitngo Wizard to help you learn correct play. Such programs will be able to instantaneously determine the calling ranges for the remaining players at which moving all-in becomes -$EV, and from these you will simply need to decide whether you believe them to be too wide or too narrow and act accordingly. Here, however, are some basic guideline for the premium hands that we have previously discussed:

A-A to Q-Q

For 15 big blinds or less you should never fold aces and kings to players who have already moved all-in, and the circumstances would need to be exceptional for you to consider folding queens, such as multiple tight deep-stacked all-in players. You should also be prepared to move all-in with them from any position against any number of players and consider whether you might get more action with aces or kings against inexperienced opposition if you make a small or min-raise instead.

J-J and 10-10

Again you can raise all-in with these hands for 15 big blinds or less in almost all situations, and call a single all-in with them most of the time, unless the raiser is in early position and extremely tight or the effective stacks are around 15 big blinds. Against multiple all-ins you should usually fold unless the players are short-stacked, in late position or very loose as you will typically face overcards or overpairs too often for playing them to be +$EV.

9-9 to 7-7

Middle pairs are still very strong hands for moving all-in with, and benefit from the fact that you won't have to worry about how to play them postflop. For this reason you can move all-in with them when you have 15 big blinds or less from almost any position, providing that you are not at a very loose table with a lot of players left, in which case you might want to fold a hand like 7-7 under-the-gun. They are harder hands to call all-in with as you will often be flipping a coin or behind, but you should still usually play against a single player when the effective stacks are 15 or fewer big blinds and they have moved all-in in late position, 10 big blinds or fewer in middle position, or seven big blinds or fewer in early position. If you are in the blinds and have chips committed already or have more chips than your opponent you should also relax these guidelines slightly.

6-6 to 2-2

Small pairs are good hands to move all-in with in late position with 15 big blinds or less, in middle position with 10 big blinds or fewer, or when you are short-stacked with seven big blinds or fewer in any position. They benefit from the fact that you will not have to make difficult postflop decisions, but when called you will usually be either flipping a coin or a long way behind a higher pair. For this reason you should not usually call an all-in with these hands unless you are in the big blind and are getting good pot odds or facing an aggressive small blind with less that 10 big blinds.

A-K

You should almost always be prepared to move all-in or call a single all-in with A-K in the late game, as it is a powerhouse hand and will usually be dominating a weaker ace or flipping a coin against a lower pair. However, if two or more players with around 15 blinds are already all-in and you have a similar stack to them, you may want to consider folding if one or both is in early position or extremely tight.

A-Q

Again, this is a powerful hand that you should almost always move all-in with, and you should usually call a single all-in with it unless your opponent is in early position, the effective stacks are around 15 big blinds and he is extremely tight. Against multiple all-ins you should usually fold it unless the players are short-stacked.

A-J and A-10

These are strong hands to move all-in with in most situations unless you are in very early position at a very loose table with a stack of close to 15 big blinds, in which case A-10o may be marginal. However, you should be more cautious about calling all-ins with them when the effective stacks are 10 big blinds or more if your opponent is very tight or in early position. In late position and against aggressive players or with shorter effective stacks, you should usually call or reraise all-in with them, however, as you are more likely to dominate weaker aces or other hands, and this is even more true when in the blinds and being offered attractive pot odds.

A-9 to A-2

When moving all-in a suited 'rag' ace has only fractionally more value than an unsuited one (for example, A-9s has similar value to A-10o) and so they should be considered in one category. They are good hands to move all-in with for 15 big blinds or less from the small blind, 10 big blinds or less in late position, seven big blinds or less in mid position, or in any position when you have five big blinds or less. However, playing them in other situations is not advisable as you will often be called by A-10+ or high pairs and be dominated. You should take the value of your kicker into consideration when you have a medium stack or are against loose players and expect to get called by weaker aces or medium pairs, although when deeper stacked and against tight players this is less significant as they will rarely call you with medium aces. You should also not call all-in with them very often unless you are in the big blind and are getting good pot odds, or the all-in has come from an aggressive player in the small blind.

Broadway hands (K-10+, Q-10+, J-10)

These are strong all-in hands (suited or not) and should be played when you are in the small blind with 15 big blinds or less, late position with 12 big blinds or less, in mid-position with eight big blinds or less, or in any position with six big blinds or less as they are less likely to be dominated when called than small pairs or weak aces (although you should consider their strength and suitedness in marginal situations). Because they are rarely ahead of an all-in player's range, however, they should not be called with unless you are in the big blind and are getting excellent pot odds, or are against a very aggressive small blind with 12 big blinds or less (although in this instance you should still only call with stronger broadway hands like K-Q, K-J and Q-Js).

Suited connectors

These hands play well against all-in calling ranges (for example 8-7s still has almost 40% equity against A-K) and can be moved all-in with when you have 15 big blinds or less in the small blind, or when you have 10 or less big blinds in late position. However, they should not usually be played when your stack is lower than five big blinds as you will have little fold equity and will often get called by the big blind with high-card hands like K-7 or Q-9 that have better all-in equity. Similarly, because you will often be losing even to steal hands you should not usually call all-ins with them unless in the big blind and getting excellent odds.

Trash hands

When you are on the button with a stack of 5-10 big blinds you may also want to move all-in with some hands that are slightly weaker than those above like rag kings or unsuited connectors, and if you in the small blind and everyone has folded to you then you can push with a wide range of hands if you have this stack size and the big blind is relatively tight. This is because he will not be able to call with many hands for ICM reasons, and you are not risking much to win the blinds, plus you will still have some equity even if you are called.

Assigning hand ranges to all-in players

Earlier we discussed how opponents should be assigned hand ranges and how these can be expressed as a percentage of all possible hands. When players move all-in ahead of you or you move all-in and there are players still left to act, being able to do this accurately is essential so that you can make good decisions or get reliable recommendations from an ICM calculator. For this reason we will now look at some common hand ranges that you might want to move all-in with or assign to players who have moved all-in before you in the late game[4]:

Top 4% of hands (10-10, A-Q+)

This range would be appropriate for moving all-in with in any position with 15 big blinds or less and calling an all-in from all but tight early position players with close to 15 big blinds.

---

[4] Note that these hand ranges are determined using game theory as opposed to ranking each hand's performance against a random hand and are approximated to the nearest %.

Top 7% of hands (8-8+, A-Jo+, A-10s+)

Again, this range would be appropriate for moving all-in with in most late game situations, but should only be used as a calling range against players in late position, those with 10 big blinds or less in middle position or those with eight big blinds or less in early position.

Top 11% of hands (4-4+, A-9o+, A-8s+, K-Qs)

This is a good range for moving all-in in late position with any stack size, with 10 big blinds or less in mid-position or with six big blinds or less in any position. However, it should only be used as a calling range in the big blind against players with 15 big blinds or less in the small blind, eight big blinds or less in late position and six big blinds or less elsewhere.

Top 15% of hands (3-3+, A-7o+, A-4s+, K-10s+)

This is a good late position or short-stacked all-in range, but should only be used as a calling range in the big blind against an aggressive small blind with 12 big blinds or less or against a player in any position with six big blinds or less.

Top 23% of hands (2-2+, A-2+, K-Jo+, K-9s+, Q-Js)

This is also a good late position or short-stacked pushing range, but you would need to be in the big blind getting good pot odds or against a very aggressive small blind with 10 big blinds or less to consider calling with it.

Top 50% of hands (2-2+, A-2+, K-2+, Q-4o+, Q-2s+, J-8o+, J-5s+, 10-9o, 10-7s+, 9-8s)

This would be a reasonable range to move all-in with from the small blind against a solid big blind when you have 12 big blinds or less in most situations. You would only call with such a range getting excellent pot odds in the big blind.

Playing against limpers and limping with high blinds

We started this chapter by looking at why moving all-in or folding is an optimal strategy when playing with high blinds, and why it is particularly effective in the late stages of a sitngo and beyond. However, not all players understand this and therefore it is important to consider how to adjust to players who limp in the late stages of sitngos. These can be divided between those who limp on the small blind when it is folded around to them, and those who will open-limp elsewhere, and between players who are habitual limpers due to inexperience and those who will use the tactic more intelligently and try to trap with big hands.

Whichever groups such players fall into, however, the most important way of determining the correct strategy is to consider their limping range and then their range for calling a raise or an all-in from another player. When a player limps on the small blind after everyone else has folded and you are the big blind, you should consider what type of player they are and whether you have seen them do this before. For example, against a passive small blind limper who has done this before you should usually move all-in with a wide range (unless you believe they have a wide range for calling your raise as well) since they will typically fold.

However, against a stronger sitngo player who rarely limps you should be extremely cautious about moving all-in (especially if they are likely to view you as aggressive), since you will often find yourself called by a very strong hand. An exception here, however, is if you have played very passively in the blinds against this player previously and suspect that they may be looking to take a cheap flop, in which case you should be more inclined to move all-in and deny them the opportunity.

Players who open limp in other positions are much rarer in the high blind stages of sitngos and typically will be weaker. Against them you need to consider their hand ranges for calling your all-in and not make the mistake of trying to push out loose-passive players with marginal hands, because you will often be called. Remember that close all-in situations are a disaster for you in the late stages of sitngos, and that whilst they may be caused by other players making bad calls, when you move all-in it is up to you to adjust your hand ranges beforehand to allow for this and avoid such situations.

Against players who frequently limp and then fold to an all-in or when there are multiple limpers, however, you can raise with a much wider range, as even when you are called there will be some overlay to compensate.

We have already considered why limping yourself is not generally recommended, but there are some very exceptional circumstances in which it might be acceptable, such as in the small blind against a passive player in the big blind. Here you will be getting 3-1 pot odds to call and see the flop (assuming that the big blind checks), which may be more profitable than risking a costly all-in with a marginal hand, particularly if the big blind is loose-passive. This approach will allow you to keep the pot small and you should often be able to steal it with a bet on the flop or later, even if you don't make anything. Limping in the small blind is also acceptable with very strong hands like big pairs against over-aggressive players who will automatically try to punish you by raising from the big blind, since you will only have to catch them with a monster hand occasionally to show a profit.

ICM considerations for late game play

Because in the late game you will primarily be playing hands all-in when you are involved, it becomes easier to quantify the effects of your decisions on your $EV by using ICM. We saw that in the early game it was -$EV to call all-in in a coin-flip situation as equity leaks away to the other players, and as more players are eliminated and the bubble draws closer the penalty for being all-in in marginal situations increases. For example, with six players left and equal stacks the situation is:

Player	Stack Size	Tournament Equity ($EV)
Player 1	2500	$166.67
Player 2	2500	$166.67
Player 3	2500	$166.67
Player 4	2500	$166.67
Player 5	2500	$166.66
Player 6	2500	$166.66

However, if two players are involved in an all-in hand and one is eliminated this changes to:

Player	Stack Size	Tournament Equity ($EV)
Player 1	2500	$178.33
Player 2	2500	$178.33
Player 3	2500	$178.33
Player 4	2500	$178.34
Player 5	5000	$286.67

This makes the percentage favourite an all-in player would now need to be to show a profit in $EV terms (discounting blinds and antes):

$$x\% = (166.67/286.67) * 100 = 58.14\%$$

Therefore as more players are eliminated the remaining players should become increasingly averse to playing all-in with marginal hands, and should tighten their calling ranges accordingly since any confrontation automatically benefits the other players. However, as a result of this, they should also widen their all-in ranges to take advantage of other players behaving in the same way. This effect, and the strategy adjustments necessary to take advantage of it, are most pronounced on the bubble, which we will consider in the next section.

A note on antes

We have previously talked about the all-in zone as measured by number of big blinds, but on sites where antes are introduced as the blinds increase it is important that you include the dead money they create in calculations you make about pushing ranges. For example, in a game where the blinds are 100/200/a25 and six players remain, there are 450 chips in the pot rather than the 300 that would be in there if no antes were in place, increasing the amount in the middle by 50%.

For this reason, when considering pushing all-in in a game with antes in play it is much more correct to think of them as increasing the size of the blinds and reducing the average stack (although there will still be differences when pot odds are considered). For example, in the situation above a player in late position with 1800 chips would do far better to push with a range that assumes the blinds are 150/300 with no antes and that he has six big blinds remaining rather than that the blinds are 100/200 and ignore the presence of antes altogether.

In actuality, however, it is even better for the aggressor to have antes in place and smaller blinds than the same amount of chips but with blinds only, since the player in the big blind will have reduced pot odds to call, having put less money in the pot initially. For example, if the player with 1800 chips pushes on the button then a deeper-stacked player will be calling 1500 to win 2250 with blinds of 150/300 in the big blind, but with antes in place and blinds of 100/200/a25 he would now be calling 1575 to win 2225 (assuming the all-in player must post his ante from a starting stack of 1800).

For this reason, when there are antes in place a player can push more a few more hands than if the corresponding amount of chips were just posted by the blinds, and, in cases where he is short-stacked and his opponent is too, quite a few more. Continuing the above example, if the button only had 900 chips to move all-in with there would be 1350 in the pot, and with blinds of 150/300 and no antes the big blind would be calling 600 for odds of over 2-1, making it an almost automatic call. However, with blinds of 100/200/a25, he would now be calling 675 to win 1325 for odds of less than 2-1, and if those 675 chips are a significant percentage of his stack then this could be prove crucial in creating fold equity.

Chapter Six

On the Bubble

Introducing the bubble

Most sitngo (and tournament) players are familiar with the concept of the bubble, which is the point at which there is only one more elimination needed before the money positions are reached. This is the key point in sitngo play, and your decisions at this stage will have a huge impact on your overall ROI. It is also the point at which ICM considerations are the most important, since there is such a large jump in prize money between fourth and third place in the standard 50%/30%/20% structure.

We will look at topics including ICM based strategies for bubble play when the blinds are high, and strategies for when the blinds are lower and you can still make smaller raises, or reraise other players with fold equity. We will also look at how stack sizes play a defining role in correct strategy at this stage, and how you should play based on your overall standing and the positions of other players at the table as well as their understanding of ICM strategies.

The sitngo player's dilemma – hang on for third or play to win?

As full table sitngos usually have a 50%/30%/20% prize structure, most players realise early in their sitngo careers that they face a dilemma at the bubble stage – should they try to survive for guaranteed third place money (which is almost twice the entry fees paid and a reasonable profit), or should they gamble and aim to secure the win for half of the entire prize pool?

This is a complex question to answer, as there are situations in which playing conservatively and waiting for the bubble to burst is entirely correct, and others in which you should play aggressively and aim for the win. Therefore, the correct approach to bubble play (as in all poker situations) is to maximise your $EV depending on your situation, which may require you to make apparently risky all-in moves in some situations or extremely tight folds in others.

In order to do this you will need to have a very close understanding of ICM principles and strategies and how winning and losing all-in hands in certain situations affects your $EV as opposed to your cEV, since it is on the bubble that these two values are most divergent. We will therefore begin by looking at how an all-in on the bubble affects the $EV of all the players still in the tournament.

ICM considerations for bubble play

Most sitngo players understand intuitively that they can move all-in on the bubble with far more hands that they can call all-in with, since when two players are involved in an all-in confrontation it immediately benefits the players who are not involved, because they are now likely to make the money without taking any risks themselves. However, most sitngo players also tend to underestimate the extent to which this is true and are often biased towards calling too much and not moving all-in enough.

In order to understand how correct hand ranges should be determined for moving all-in or calling all-in, we need to start by considering the effect of being all-in on the bubble on the $EV of all the players in the game. We can use ICM to quantify this effect by considering the same 10-player $100 tournament we looked at earlier, where there are now four equal-stacked players remaining. Ignoring the presence of blinds and antes, it will look like:

Player	Stack Size	Tournament Equity ($EV)
Player 1	3750	$250
Player 2	3750	$250
Player 3	3750	$250
Player 4	3750	$250

However if Players 3 and 4 go all-in and Player 3 wins the hand then the bubble will have burst, which changes the situation to:

Player	Stack Size	Tournament Equity ($EV)
Player 1	3750	$308.33
Player 2	3750	$308.33
Player 3	7500	$383.34

Here the leakage of equity to the other players is massive, since although they still have the same amount of chips, they are now guaranteed $200 for third place because of the elimination. Because of this, Player 3's percentage chance of winning the all-in hand would need to be far higher for him to break even in $EV terms, since he is essentially creating a freeroll for Players 1 and 2 whilst risking elimination himself:

$$x\% = (\$250/\$383.33) * 100 = 65.22\%$$

Therefore if a player has already moved all-in on the bubble and the stack sizes are similar you will need a very strong hand to call all-in in order to offset this effect, and you will need to fold many good hands that you would call with in other situations.

Of course, on the bubble the blinds will usually be very high and if you are in the big blind you may be getting attractive pot odds, so the true figure will be slightly less in practice, depending on your position at the table, that of the all-in player and the size of the blinds and stacks. For example, with stacks of 3750 and blinds of 200/400 we can calculate the following minimum win percentages for certain situations:

Situation	$EV fold	$EV call/win	Win % needed
Call in BB vs. B/CO	$232.66	$387.03	60.11%
Call in BB vs. SB	$232.30	$383.33	60.60%
Call in SB*	$242	$390.70	61.94%
Call on Button*	$250	$394.27	63.41%

* Here we assume that the remaining players fold.

As you can see, these numbers are still all significantly higher than they were in the early stages of the sitngo because of the bubble effect, and so, even allowing for pot odds, players should not be calling all-in with many hands. We will now look at this effect from another perspective and consider how it affects the hand ranges that players should be prepared to move all-in with on the bubble.

Moving all-in on the bubble

ICM shows us that when all players have similar stack sizes on the bubble an all-in confrontation can be disastrous for one player's $EV unless they have a very big edge. We can now examine how this influences correct strategy in high blind situations where players are frequently able to pick up the blinds and antes by moving all-in with a wide hand range and forcing opponents to call all-in and risk elimination if they want to play a hand.

Consider the same $100 sitngo as above, this time with the button on Player 4 and the blinds at 200/400 (note that $EV is calculated before the blinds are posted):

Player	Stack Size	Tournament Equity ($EV)
Player 1 (SB)	3750	$250
Player 2 (BB)	3750	$250
Player 3	3750	$250
Player 4 (Button)	3750	$250

Now let's assume that both Player 3 and Player 4 fold, leaving Player 1 to act in the small blind against Player 2 (who is a tight-aggressive player) in the big blind. Limping is not an option, because Player 2 may raise with a wide range, so his decision is restricted to moving all-in or folding. What percentage of his hand range should Player 1 move all-in with?

Using an ICM calculator we can determine that if the Player 2 calls only with the top 14% of all hands (4-4+, A-8o+, A-4s+, K-Js+) then it will be correct for Player 1 to move all-in with 100% of his hands, because he will win the blinds so often that this will easily compensate for the times he is called and eliminated.

The question therefore is how often should Player 2 fold? Well, even if Player 1 tells Player 2 that he will move all-in with 100% of his range Player 2 can still only profitably call with around 12.5% of hands (6-6+, A-7s+, A-10o+, K-Qo and K-10s+) as in doing so he must still risk elimination. By definition therefore Player 1's play is unexploitable and he should always move all-in with 100% of his range here, assuming that Player 2 acts in his own best interest.

A note on assuming optimal opposition, and accounting for sub-optimal opposition

The above example shows a situation where it is assumed that both players behave optimally (i.e. they always play to maximize their own $EV). However, in practice you will rarely encounter players who manage exactly that even at the highest limits. Therefore when considering situations like moving all-in with a very weak hand you need to consider the opponents you are up against and whether they are likely to make calls that could be harmful to both of you. For example, in the above scenario, although moving all-in from the small blind with 3-2o would be correct against an expert sitngo player, against a player calling with a wide range it would be disastrous.

The reasons for the big blind making a bad call could be many, including ignorance of ICM principles, frustration with a very aggressive player constantly moving all-in from the small blind, or even a 'spite call' from one strong player against another. However, it is your responsibility to assess an opponent's calling range when deciding whether to move all-in or fold and adjust accordingly, and you should not berate them for your errors in this department.

Assessing stack sizes, blind structures and seating positions

So far we have only considered bubble situations where all players have equal stacks, but in real life this will rarely be the case and situations will change rapidly. Therefore it is important that you pay close attention not only to your opponents and how they are playing, but also the exact make-up of the bubble situation you are in.

This might mean monitoring your overall standing in the sitngo and how many rounds of blinds you can go before you must make an all-in move to protect your stack size; whether your nearest rivals are going to have to take the blinds before you if you are short-stacked; when the blinds will rise and who will face the first increase; or whether there is a player whose position could cause you problems such as a big stack who is moving all-in every hand before you and denying you the opportunity to steal.

Much of this sounds trivial, but keeping an observant eye on the situation will often help you with forward planning and decision-making in situations where ICM $EV decisions are close but other factors may lead you to want to make or avoid a marginal all-in move. We will now look at a few of the common situations that occur on the bubble and how you should play in them.

When all stacks are similar in size

As we saw above, when all players are close to equal in chips on the bubble, a player moving all-in has a lot of leverage, and with stacks of around 10 big blinds should usually move all-in 100% of the time from the small blind. This adds an interesting twist to the 'sitngo player's dilemma' discussed earlier, since rather than taking the view that someone will be eliminated soon and waiting for this to happen, it is almost always better for you to play aggressively in such situations to seize the chip lead.

This is because you will frequently have opportunities to make +$EV all-in moves to steal the blinds and antes when the stacks are similar, and as you develop a chip lead these opportunities will become even more frequent since you will not be eliminated even if you lose an all-in. And the more successful you are in this strategy, the more your opponents will become locked into a battle of survival, allowing you to accumulate an even larger stack which will give you a good chance of wining the sitngo outright.

To illustrate this we can continue our previous example, assuming that Player 1 correctly pushes with 100% of his hands in the small blind against Player 2 in the big blind, and that Player 2 folds and the bubble continues (which will happen 87.5% of the time if he calls optimally), making the new situation:

Player	Stack Size	Tournament Equity ($EV)
Player 1	4150	$266.72
Player 2 (SB)	3350	$232.30
Player 3 (BB)	3750	$250.49
Player 4	3750	$250.49

At this stage Player 1 has taken a slight chip lead, but it will already be advantageous to his pushing range since now he cannot be eliminated by a call from another player. If Player 4 folds here, then Player 1 now has the opportunity to move all-in again, and should still do so with a very wide range and with any two cards if the blinds will only call with the top 7% of all hands (8-8+, A-Jo+, A-10s+). If both blinds fold, which they usually will, and the bubble continues then the new situation will be:

Player	Stack Size	Tournament Equity ($EV)
Player 1	4750	$289.56
Player 2	3150	$224.20
Player 3 (SB)	3350	$234.10
Player 4 (BB)	3750	$252.14

Now Player 1 has opened up a lead of 1000 chips against the field and will still have a legitimate chance of making a comeback even if he loses an all-in. Because of this he can continue pushing a wide range if the other players are likely to now start waiting for one of their number to be eliminated. In fact, if they only call with the top 5% of hands (9-9+, A-Q+) Player 1 can move all-in with any two cards here. Thus in just three hands Player 1 could establish a dominating stack:

Player	Stack Size	Tournament Equity ($EV)
Player 1 (BB)	5350	$309.87
Player 2	3150	$226.78
Player 3	3150	$226.78
Player 4 (SB)	3350	$236.57

We will now examine how being successful in this strategy may further benefit a player on the bubble by massively increasing his overall chance of winning the sitngo.

When you have a dominating stack

A dominating stack is one which can move all-in on the bubble frequently and with virtual impunity, since the other players will rarely be able to call and even when they do and it loses this will not significantly harm its owners' $EV, as he will still have a playable stack remaining. Generally this should mean having sufficiently more chips than the next largest stack to be able to go back to playing a standard short-stack strategy, which roughly translates to an additional five big blinds.

Let us continue our example above, assuming the other players are now playing tighter and waiting for one of their number to bust so that they are guaranteed prize money. If all players fold around to Player 1 in the big blind, giving him a walk, then on the next hand the stacks will be:

Player	Stack Size	Tournament Equity ($EV)
Player 1 (SB)	5550	$316.25
Player 2 (BB)	3150	$227.92
Player 3	3150	$227.92
Player 4	3150	$227.91

Now Player 1 is back in the small blind and Player 2 in the big blind, but this time he has 2400 more chips than Player 2, making his decision to move all-in with any hand even easier since he will still have a reasonable stack left if he loses. If Player 2 only calls with the top 22% of all hands (3-3+, A-3o+, A-2s+, K-Jo+, K-10s+, Q-Js), then this will be +$EV, which should usually be the case.

Assuming that Player 1 continues to move all-in liberally and collect the blinds, his job of amassing a stack that can go on to win the sitngo once the bubble bursts becomes easier and easier. He is risking less chips to win the blinds, as the other player's stacks are eroded, and the bigger the lead he achieves the less significant losing an all-in becomes. In fact, with a very large stack and three very short stacks he should still be the chip leader even after losing an all-in and would be able to go straight back to accumulating chips again.

Of course, the other stacks will rarely be exactly equal, but in such situations you will be able to apply even more pressure to the second and third place stacks who will not be able to call all-in with many hands when there are players behind them in the standings who are more likely to be eliminated. This will especially be the case if there is a 'micro-stack' (i.e. one which cannot even survive the next round of blinds without being all-in) present, at which point the other players must fold virtually every hand until that player is eliminated.

As is obvious, however, the bubble circumstances will gradually change and the other players will become more inclined to call an all-in as their stack sizes diminish, whether out of necessity due to their shrinking stack and the rising blinds, as a response to your aggressive strategy, or out of sheer frustration or ignorance. Whichever, you will need to remain aware of the changing circumstances and eventually start to adjust by moving all-in with fewer hands in some circumstances if players are unable or unwilling to pass.

When one of your opponents has a dominating stack

When one of your opponents has a dominating stack, your strategy should depend on their behaviour, your chip position relative to the remaining two players, and the arrangement of stacks at the table. If the big stack is moving all-in frequently in front of you there may be very little you can do apart from remain patient, wait for +$EV calling hands, and consider which of the remaining players will face elimination first, but often players with a big stack will not play as aggressively as they should and you may have more opportunities to push all-in yourself and even overtake the big stack eventually.

In the situation where you are up against an aggressive big stack, your stack size relative to that of the other players (and accounting for the order in which players take the blinds) will be key. If you are comfortably ahead of the third and fourth place players you should not be looking to play many hands, and usually move all-in when you do to avoid giving the big stack any fold equity against you if he is an aggressive player and likely to reraise you with a wide range.

However, if you are the lowest stack or in close competition with one or both of the other players you will need to pay close attention to your stack sizes in terms of big blinds, the order in which players must take the blinds and whether they are likely to increase soon. Your main goal at this stage is to stay ahead of the pack and force another player to risk elimination before you, whilst maintaining the fold equity and chip position of your stack by making +$EV pushes when the opportunity arises, but avoiding unnecessary risks and confrontations.

One more thing to note is that, in this kind of situation, you should be more inclined to call an all-in against another short stack than against the big stack, since doubling through the big stack will not burst the bubble. Despite this, however, your calling range should still be narrow if there are three short stacks, since a confrontation will benefit the third short-stacked player substantially in terms of equity leakage. If you are faced with a close decision against the big stack, however, you should also consider whether calling all-in and winning will make you the big stack, as you will then be able to gather additional chips by virtue of that position of dominance.

When you have a short stack or micro-stack

When you are extremely short on chips and in last position of the remaining players, you will need to look for the best opportunity to put your chips in based on the stack size you have remaining. If you have a stack of greater than five big blinds then you will still be able to go through the next blinds and retain some fold equity. However, you should be wary of letting your stack fall below 50% of the next smallest stack since this will make a comeback more difficult, both because you will have less fold equity against them and because if you do double through them they will still have a playable stack.

With a stack of below five big blinds, you will usually want to look for a situation to move all-in before the next big blind hits you. With 3.5-5 big blinds this is because your stack will still have some fold equity and maintaining it will be invaluable on the bubble, which may even make a slightly -$EV all-in correct according to ICM if you are under-the-gun and in last place, as ICM does not take into account the impact of the big blind on the next hand. You should also particularly look to move all-in against the big blind of players who are under pressure and cannot call simply due to pot odds. With 1.5-3.5 big blinds it is because you will usually be committed to calling all-in in the big blind with any two cards and therefore it is almost always better to make a stand prior to that, unless you really find no playable hand or situation.

Note, however, that when you have a micro-stack of 1.5 big blinds or less even if you do double up you will not usually get back to being above 5 big blinds and will therefore have to look for another hand to play before the big blind reaches you, or be committed in the big blind if you doubled up when under-the-gun. In this situation you should therefore be more inclined to let the big blind hit you unless you find a hand that is at least quite a bit above average, since you will always be committed to calling in the big blind with a stack this size and face no tough decisions, and if you survive it then you will have another round to look for a better hand to commit your chips with.

With a very short stack you should also look for situations where you have at least a reasonable hand and another player's raise offers you protection from playing against more than one player and good pot odds. For example, consider the following situation:

Player	Stack Size	Tournament Equity ($EV)
Player 1	8400	$395.07
Player 2	600	$68.91
Player 3 (SB)	3000	$268.01
Player 4 (BB)	3000	$268.01

If the blinds are 200/400 and Player 1 moves all-in here, then you should be prepared to call with a wide range since you will have to take the big blind in two hands anyway, and here the blinds are likely to fold leaving you getting 2-1 pot odds against one player. In fact, if Player 1 is moving all-in every hand, you should be prepared to call with a very wide range since the equity boost you will get from winning will take your $EV to $167.31 (assuming no-one else calls), and you will suddenly have a playable stack of 1800 again with some fold equity for the next hand.

Attacking your nearest rivals

As we have seen, unless you have a dominating stack you may well find yourself in a three-way competition to avoid being the bubble player, and just as you should be more inclined to tangle with one of those players than the big stack in an all-in situation, so you should also be more inclined to attack their big blind with your all-ins rather than that of the big-stacked player. The same ICM reasons apply here, but against a similarly sized stack you will also have additional fold equity, since that player will be eliminated or severely damaged by calling you and losing, and if you steal their blind you will have gained the two-fold benefit of not only increasing your own stack but decreasing theirs.

This idea may seem obvious, but it can apply more pertinently when you are in an extreme situation where the blinds are very high and you must move all-in before they next hit you in order to maintain a stack with fold equity. In such a situation where you might have a stack size of 3.5-5 big blinds, moving in against another similarly-sized stack's big blind with a mediocre hand will often be superior to moving in against that of the big stack with a reasonable one. This is because in the first instance you will have significantly more fold equity, and when called will at least have created a 'me or him' situation where you should usually make the money if you win the hand, whereas in the second the big stack will be more able to call based on pot odds as he will still have chips behind and you will gain less from doubling through him.

For example, consider the following situation, with blinds of 200/400/a25:

Player	Stack Size	Tournament Equity ($EV)
Player 1	5500	$324.16
Player 2	2000	$175.84
Player 3 (SB)	5500	$324.16
Player 4 (BB)	2000	$175.84

If Player 1 folds, then Player 2 should push with a very wide range as Player 3 is unlikely to call often and Player 4 is his main competitor. In fact, if Player 3 only calls with the top 10% of all hands (5-5+, A-10o+, A-8s+, K-Qs) and Player 4 only calls with the top 22% (3-3+, A-3o+, A-2s+, K-Jo+, K-10s+, Q-Js) then Player 2 should move all-in with any two cards here according to ICM.

Calling all-in (and calling an all-in) on the bubble

At the bubble stage, moving all-in is usually a superior play to calling all-in, but there are still many situations where it becomes mathematically correct to call all-in (or call another player's all-in) according to ICM. These mostly occur when you have a very strong hand or a big stack and a reasonable hand that you can afford to risk an all-in with.

However, you may also call all-in when the pot odds you are getting are overwhelming because either you or another player is short-stacked and you are in the big blind, or because you are in the big blind and calling will enable you to eliminate or cripple an opponent and this is a significant advantage to you.

When the best course of action is not obvious, you should consider your opponent's likely hand range, as well as the stack sizes and the impact your decision will have on the outcome of the bubble. For example, when you and another player are competing to avoid the bubble against two larger stacks, and the other small stack moves all-in against your big blind, you should often call with marginal hands like small pairs, face cards and weaker aces if you are both short-stacked. This is because his pushing range is likely to be wider against your blind that against the big stack's, you are getting good pot odds and calling creates a 'me or him' situation where you will likely make the money if you win the hand, whereas if you fold you will be in fourth place and the favourite to bubble anyway.

For example, continuing our example above, with blinds of 200/400/a25:

Player	Stack Size	Tournament Equity ($EV)
Player 1	5500	$324.16
Player 2	2000	$175.84
Player 3 (SB)	5500	$324.16
Player 4 (BB)	2000	$175.84

If Player 1 folds, Player 2 moves all-in and Player 3 folds, then Player 4 should call with a very wide range to avoid a situation where he has 1400 chips left after posting the small blind on the next hand and Player 1 has 2600. In fact, if Player 2 always moves all-in here then Player 4 should call with about the top two-thirds or all hands, and if he moves all-in with any better than average hand then about the top 33%.

Cooperative vs. non-cooperative bubble strategies

Because the penalty for bubbling in a sitngo is so severe, and this allows the big stack to play very aggressively to accumulate chips, there are some situations in which it may be correct for smaller stacks to deviate from a standard all-in or fold strategy in order to co-operate in ending the bubble faster if another player has a micro-stack. This strategy is know as 'implicit collusion', and whilst explicit collusion like discussing hands and strategies or soft playing is strictly against the rules in tournament poker, situations where two players will silently check down a hand or play more passively in order to create the maximum probability of eliminating a third player are common.

For example, consider the following situation in a 10-player $100 tournament where the blinds are 200/400 and the big blind is all-in for his remaining chips:

Player	Stack Size	Tournament Equity ($EV)
Player 1	11000	$441.39
Player 2	1800	$244.80
Player 3 (SB)	1800	$244.80
Player 4 (BB)	400	$69.01

If Player 1 folds and Player 2 limps, then it would be correct for Player 3 to limp from the small blind with a very wide range and only raise all-in with his strongest hands in order to try and create the highest probability of Player 4 being eliminated. Of course, it is true that if he does raise all-in then Player 1 will often fold, however with high blinds and the presence of a dominating stack which has leverage over the table Player 3 should usually be more concerned about ending the bubble quickly than trying to apply leverage to Player 2. This is because the $EV gained from allowing Player 2 the opportunity to win the hand and end the bubble is usually greater than that gained by forcing him out and playing heads-up against the micro-stack but risking its continuation.

Therefore in some situations playing cooperatively can be beneficial in sitngos, but most players who do this generally take it too far. For example, in the above situation, you would not want to take this approach with stronger hands like 8-8+, A-10+ which have good equity against one opponent already. Similarly, there are many situations in which non-cooperative bubble play is by far the most profitable strategy (even though some old-fashioned players will demur when they see it being used).

For example, in the above hand it would actually be in Player 1's interest to keep the bubble going so that he can reduce the stacks of Players 2 and 3 even further whilst they wait for the micro-stack to be eliminated. He should therefore never be willing to limp and co-operate here, and should in fact move all-in with a very wide range to force the other players out as they will not be able to call and risk elimination with many hands. This will usually allow him to play all-in against the big blind with 200 dead chips already in the pot, with the result either being him winning both those chips and Player 4's remaining chips or the continuation of the bubble, which is not a bad result either since he can then go on exploiting it.

Manipulating all-in situations when players are short-stacked

There are a few situations when you or an opponent are short-stacked where you can manipulate a likely all-in situation to potentially create additional equity against inattentive or inexperienced opponents. This applies when you are short-stacked and committed to a hand but your opponent may be caused to overlook this fact and fold incorrectly, or when an opponent should be committed to a hand but you allow them the opportunity to make an incorrect fold.

An example of the first case is when you have a stack size which is below the point at which you can expect to have fold equity when raising all-in against the big blind, but you can still make a standard sized raise that commits you but may lead the big blind to miss the fact that you have few chips left behind. For example, consider the following situation with blinds of 200/400/a25:

Player	Stack Size	Tournament Equity ($EV)
Player 1	3900	$441.39
Player 2	1275	$244.80
Player 3 (SB)	3800	$244.80
Player 4 (BB)	6025	$69.01

If Player 1 folds and Player 2 moves all-in he can expect to be called by the big blind with almost any two cards. However, if he raises to 1200 then an inattentive big blind who is multi-tabling and must make swift decisions may fail to spot this and fold incorrectly believing him to have a much deeper stack in total. Of course, this will not work even the majority of the time, but it costs you nothing extra since you are always committed for the extra 75 chips and so even a 1% success rate would be very good for your long term $EV.

Similarly, when you face a very short stack who is committed in the blinds and have a marginal hand you may want to try and create fold equity by using a variation of the 'stop and go' play. For example consider the following situation, again with blinds of 200/400/a25:

Player	Stack Size	Tournament Equity ($EV)
Player 1	4900	$319.99
Player 2	2500	$233.33
Player 3 (SB)	6800	$362.48
Player 4 (BB)	800	$84.20

If both blinds fold and Player 3 is left up against Player 4, who is committed to calling any raise as he has over 50% of his stack in the big blind, then with a marginal holding like 6-5o it would cost him nothing extra to flat call and then automatically bet the flop if the big blind checks. In this instance, if the big blind moves all-in it will still be correct to call the raise, but if the big blind checks and misses the flop, then Player 3 will often win the pot without having to improve, because Player 4 will usually have to fold. Since two unpaired cards will usually fail to make a pair on the flop you will therefore gain equity from the times that you both miss but your opponent folds a better unimproved hand.

Of course, this play will not work often and is only likely to succeed against inexperienced players, but it costs you nothing extra to make it and 6-5o will always be behind your opponents all-in calling range, so even if the benefit is only fractional then this is still free equity. One additional benefit in the above example is that if this play succeeds then it would also keep the bubble going with a newly created micro-stack, which would be an ideal situation for the big stack to exploit.

Planning for and manipulating blind increases

Since at the bubble stage most stacks will be under severe blind pressure, it is important to know when the blinds are going to rise and how much the next big blind is likely to cost so that you can plan ahead. For example, this might mean making more aggressive plays beforehand if you need to accumulate chips in order to survive the next blind increase or maintain a stack with fold equity, or fewer aggressive ones if the new level will remove a shorter stack's fold equity or commit them to calling all-in in the next big blind and you have a stack that can survive until they must risk elimination.

A more controversial topic is whether you should attempt to manipulate who takes the first big blind at the new level by stalling when there is only a short amount of time left in the current one. This could be very important to the outcome of the bubble if it gains you extra hands at a new level where there are more chips to win when you move all-in, or if you and another player are short-stacked and the increased big blind will cost then a significant portion of their stack.

Since stalling is not technically illegal and falls into a grey area it is up to player to decide themselves what they consider fair game and where to draw the line. However, if you are going to make stalling when the blinds are about to rise a part of your game, it is certainly true that you do not want it to be obvious as this may result in other players returning the favour or targeting you in other ways that will reduce your $EV.

As a guide therefore, whilst waiting a few extra seconds for the blinds to rise in a crucial bubble spot is probably acceptable (and no-one will ever be able to say for certain), using up your entire time bank in such a situation, or consistently stalling to make sure you have the button or that the short stack always suffers when the blinds increase is taking things too far.

When the stacks are still deep on the bubble

Sometimes in a sitngo you will reach the bubble quickly with the blinds still at quite a low level where most players have stacks of 15 big blinds or more and are in a position to make raises and continuation bets, or reraise another player all-in. This might be because several players have been eliminated early by chance in a turbo event, or you are playing in a slower speed sitngo where this is naturally the case.

In such a situation the stack sizes and the behaviour of the biggest stack is key to your decisions. If you are the biggest stack then moving all-in to steal the blinds will be unnecessarily risky until players are below 15 big blinds, and you should look to make frequent smaller raises to pick them up with minimal risk until either the other stacks are reduced or the blinds rise to take the stacks below that level. At very weak-passive tables you may be able to raise the majority of hands if people are unwilling to play back at you, and if your raise is to 2.5 big blinds then you will not need to win the pot a high percentage of the time to show an immediate profit.

Playing a dominating stack when deep

If you have a dominating stack when the blinds are still low on the bubble, you should look to use the leverage you have to put other players who make standard opening raises to the test with a wide range, unless you know that they would not make a small raise without a strong hand in such a spot. This is because, many players will blindly open and fold to a reraise without consideration of bubble strategy, and against these players you should be prepared to reraise them with a very wide range of hands since the mathematics of bubble play will dissuade them from calling all-in, and particularly calling against the big stack.

For example, consider the following situation with blinds of 75/150:

Player	Stack Size	Tournament Equity ($EV)
Player 1	2500	$210
Player 2	7500	$370
Player 3 (SB)	2500	$210
Player 4 (BB)	2500	$210

If Player 1 opens to 450 then there is suddenly 675 in the pot for Player 2 to win if he can force Player 1 out by raising all-in. By doing so he risks 2500 chips but he will not be called often unless Player 1 has a very tight opening range or a very loose calling range (or one of the other players picks up a big pair). Player 2 should therefore be prepared to reraise with a wide range here since when Player 1 folds he gains around $16 in equity, and even if we assume the most extreme situation where Player 2 reraises with any two cards and is called by 10-10+, A-Q+ he only loses around $40 in equity, so Player 1 would only have to fold around 71.5% of the time or more to make this profitable.

Therefore against players who do not adjust well to the bubble and will blindly raise-fold in these situations you can reraise with almost any two cards. Even against less predictable players you should still often make this move when you have a hand with good equity against a calling range like suited connectors or one high card like an ace or king. However, you should also watch out for players who are likely to make 'hero' calls against you if you do it too often, and you should still be careful of reraising with trash hands against players who may make bad calls according to ICM, or against intelligent players who are only likely to open with very strong hands in the hope that you will reraise them.

Playing a medium stack when deep

When you have a stack that is bigger than 15 big blinds but you are not the chip leader, you will need to consider whether the big stack is likely to take the above strategy against you and act accordingly, simply folding or moving all-in with hands that you wish to play if your stack is of a sensible size, and only open-raising with hands that you can confidently call a reraise with or when the big stack has already folded. Remember that at this stage you will not be under immediate blind pressure and preservation is your best option rather than giving opponents the opportunity to exploit you, particularly if other players are likely to make mistakes like these.

With a stack of this size you will also be able to reraise all-in against players who make a standard opening raise and expect to have significant fold equity. In this situation, however, since you will have few or no chips left if you are called and lose you should be very careful about reraising with marginal hands against players who have big stacks or are likely to make loose calls. For this reason, and because most players will be inclined to open more tightly on the bubble, you should not usually make steal reraises with hands like 9-8s or K-Qo and rather wait for stronger hands like A-10+ and mid- to high pairs unless you believe you have significant fold equity.

Chapter Seven

In the Money (playing three-handed)

Introducing the 'in the money' stage

Since we are considering standard nine- and ten-handed sitngos with a payout structure of 50%/30%/20%, the 'in the money' stage is reached when three players are left and the bubble has 'burst'. We will consider how strategy changes according to ICM considerations now that players have achieved their primary goal of cashing for a guaranteed profit, and how a new three-handed tournament has effectively begun where the payout structure places the emphasis on playing to win.

Re-evaluating the payout structure

Once the bubble bursts and the money stages are reached it is important to notice that 60% of the prize money is now allocated since each player is guaranteed 20%. In effect therefore a new tournament has begun amongst the remaining three players for the remaining 40% of the prize pool, with first getting an additional 30%, second an additional 10% and third nothing extra. With this huge weighting towards finishing first, you should usually play more aggressively and aim for the win when three-handed unless there is some compelling reason to try and secure second place money first, such as being against one very large stack and one micro-stack which will soon face elimination. Again, we can determine strategy at this stage using ICM.

ICM considerations for three-handed play

Up until the bubble bursts, ICM calculations show us that the penalties for risking marginal all-ins are severe and become more so the closer to the bubble the game gets. However, with a new payout structure once the money is reached of 30%/10%/0% this effect is lessened as the biggest jump in prize money is from second to first. If we consider our $100 sitngo example at the three-handed stage, where there is an additional $400 in prize money to allocate, the situation will look like this:

Player	Stack Size	Tournament Equity ($EV)
Player 1	5000	$133.33
Player 2	5000	$133.33
Player 3	5000	$133.34

However, if two players manage to get all-in immediately the situation changes to:

Player	Stack Size	Tournament Equity ($EV)
Player 1	10,000	$233.33
Player 2	5000	$166.67

As we can see therefore, there is much less equity leakage than on the bubble and the percentage favourite you would need to be to take a coin-flip at this stage is significantly reduced compared to the bubble:

$$x\% = (\$133.33/\$233.33) * 100 = 57.14\%$$

This, coupled with the fact that the blinds will usually be very high relative to the stack sizes, means that players must re-evaluate their all-in strategy at this stage and push with a much tighter range of hands since they will be more frequently called. For example, in the above situation with three equal stacks and blinds of 300/600 the small blind would only be able to push profitably with 100% of hands if the big blind only calls with the top 21% of all hands (3-3+, A-4o+, -A-2s+, K-Jo+, K-10s+, Q-Js. However, if the big blind knows that his opponent will move all-in with any hand, then he should call with approximately the top 40% of hands. Therefore, the small blind would be making a significant error here by trying to apply an aggressive bubble strategy of moving all-in with any hand and should tighten up significantly.

Re-evaluating strategy for three-handed play

When you reach three-handed play the new payout structure means that you should be more inclined to gamble since there is less penalty for being all-in in a marginal spot, particularly if the blinds are high and afford attractive pot odds. Because of this your strategy must change whatever size of stack you have. If you were the big stack that dominated the bubble then you should now be moving all-in with less marginal hands, since your fold equity is reduced and players will be much more inclined to call you when they think that they have an edge against your range. Because of this you should only make moves that you are sure are +$EV against these wider calling ranges, unless there is one very short stack, in which case you may still aggressively target the second-place player.

If you are a short stack, and particularly if you are in danger of going below five big blinds and losing your fold equity, you must start playing aggressively straight away to maintain it and be happy to take more risks since you have achieved your primarily goal of cashing and have little to lose. As we saw with bubble play, you should still prefer to target the second place stack in order to reduce the gap between you the quickest, but you should also be more inclined to gamble by making thin calls against other players' all-ins, since with few chips and a top heavy payout structure there will be less equity leakage when you double up than with a large stack. For example, consider the following situation:

Player	Stack Size	Tournament Equity ($EV)
Player 1	7500	$185.75
Player 2	5250	$146.18
Player 3	2250	$68.07

Now if Player 3 doubles through Player 2, this changes to:

Player	Stack Size	Tournament Equity ($EV)
Player 1	7500	$183.93
Player 2	3000	$88.57
Player 3	4500	$127.50

As you can see, Player 3's stack has doubled and his equity has almost doubled too since his short stack is so precious, the payout structure is top heavy and he has managed to knock Player 2 down into third place (if he doubled through Player 1 his equity would only be $122.31). If you consider that the blinds will usually be at least 200/400 at this stage, offering additional pot odds on any call, it is clear that Player 3 should be calling all-in with a holding that is even slightly ahead of his opponent's range. For example, in the above scenario if Player 2 moves all-in from the small blind and Player 3 folds in the big blind his equity will reduce to $56.78, but if he calls it will increase to $127.50, meaning that he only has to have 44.53% equity against the small blind's range to call according to ICM.

When the stacks are still deep in three-handed play

Sometimes the stacks will still be above 15 big blinds even when you have reached three-handed play. For example, a PokerStars sitngo will sometimes reach the money with blinds of 100/200 or 100/200/a25 and an average stack of 4500. In this situation you should be making normal-sized raises and continuation bets (unless one player has a short stack) and playing a more traditional three-handed game since with most of the money going to first place the other players will have less re-stealing equity than on the bubble.

Position will also be paramount in this situation and you should be raising frequently from the button, but usually preferring to reraise all-in or fold out of position rather than call. Also, because players will now be opening more loosely, and the penalty for playing a large all-in pot is smaller, you should be more inclined to make looser reraises and resteals against other players with hands like K-Qo or 9-8s, particularly if they are your main rival or you have reason to believe that they will fold a high percentage of the time. By doing this you will either pick up additional chips when they fold, or force an all-in confrontation where if you win you will be in a strong position to go on and win the sitngo, and if you lose you still have the 20% of the prize money that you were already guaranteed.

Chapter Eight

Heads-up (playing one-on-one)

Introducing heads-up play

When only two players remain in a sitngo (known as playing heads-up) you are effectively playing a 'cash game freezeout' for the remaining prize money. We will look at how the chips in play now have a linear real money value which makes applying ICM unnecessary, and how with this new structure equity decisions become more straightforward. We will also consider how players can adopt a smallball or an all-in or fold approach to ensure success at this stage.

Playing in a 'cash game freezeout'

With two players remaining you are effectively playing a heads-up tournament for the remaining prize-money, with first place getting all of it and second nothing. Therefore ICM considerations become irrelevant at this stage, as with only one additional prize remaining your chips have a linear value as they would in a cash game (although you must still play until someone wins them all). For example, in our 10-player $1000 sitngo with payouts of $500, $300 and $200, if two players reach the heads-up stage with stacks of 4000 and 6000 it is easy to calculate their $EV. Since both players are guaranteed $300 (and third place has already been awarded

$200) there is only $200 left to play for and each player's share of that directly corresponds to their share of the 10,000 chips in play:

$$HU \ \$EV \ of \ Player \ 1 = (4000/10,000) * \$200 = \$80$$

$$HU \ \$EV \ of \ Player \ 2 = (6000/10,000) * \$200 = \$120$$

For this reason all you need to think about when heads-up is whether any play you make is +cEV, since if that is the case it will always be +$EV as well.

Smallball vs. jam or fold strategies

Usually in a full table sitngo by the time heads-up play has been reached the average stack size will have dropped to below 15 big blinds and you will not have much room for manoeuvre. For this reason it is important to make swift decisions about how to approach the match based on your opponent and the depth of stacks.

Against a very weak player and with deeper stacks you should generally apply a smallball strategy that consists of limping or making small raises and playing postflop, but with shorter stacks and against tougher opponents you should revert to an all-in or fold strategy, and against very tough players employ a game theory optimal strategy that they will not be able to exploit.

Playing smallball

With stacks of greater than 15 big blinds you will be risking a great deal to win very little by playing all-in or fold poker, and so you should tend towards limping or raising to three big blinds and continuation betting frequently for 3-4 big blinds when called and checked to. The former will allow you to control the size of the pot and outplay opponents postflop, whilst the latter will give you two chances to win the pot, and still enable you to escape with most of your stack remaining if you are checkraised or called and have no hand.

Precisely what approach you take and the frequency with which you do certain things should depend on your opponent however. With stacks of 15 big blinds or more raising to three big blinds preflop rather than moving all-in is obviously superior if your opponent will fold similar ranges of hands to both actions, but less ideal if he will now reraise you with a wider range, believing that you will fold frequently (in which case you might simply open with a tighter range and call his reraises with a wider one, or even revert to a jam or fold strategy to deny him any fold equity against you). Similarly, often limping the button to control the size of the pot is ideal against loose-passive opponents who you figure to be able to outplay later, but will not work against aggressive opponents who will raise or move all-in frequently when you do this unless you manage to trap them with big hands.

With stacks of below 15 big blinds, and especially below 10 big blinds where a jam or fold strategy becomes most effective, you should only employ smallball tactics against highly exploitable players such as those who are very loose-passive and you have a big skill edge over postflop when you limp in, or those who are very tight and will fold a wide range of hands to a small raise, making it unnecessary to risk your whole stack to win the blinds. Of course, the lower the effective stacks get the more often you should simply revert to all-in or fold poker, since after a certain point you will be committed to calling an all-in anyway if you make a small raise, and you should usually therefore just move all-in yourself first if you intend to play.

Jam or fold

When you have less than 15 big blinds and are against a tough or unknown opponent (or if you yourself are inexperienced) you should usually adopt a jam (i.e. all-in) or fold strategy that forces then to commit all their chips if they want to play a hand or give up the blinds if they fold. This might be based on your opponent's tendencies if they are very exploitable (e.g. someone who folds too much and doesn't call enough) or on a game theory optimal strategy that will combat tougher heads-up opponents who have a good understanding of such strategy themselves.

The latter is a situation that has been addressed by Bill Chen and Jerrod Ankenman, who have calculated jam (i.e. all-in) or fold tables allowing for game theory optimal play when heads-up with high blinds, which are reproduced below from their groundbreaking work *The Mathematics of Poker*[5]. Here you will see one table for playing when you are the attacker in the small blind, and one for playing when you are the defender in the big blind, with a complete list of all hold'em hands and numerical values for each. These are the maximum stack sizes for moving all-in or calling all-in with that hand before blinds are posted, with all hands that have a value greater than 20 big blinds simply being marked 'J' for Jam (i.e. all-in) or 'C' for call, indicating that with a stack of 20 big blinds or fewer you should always play them:

Defender (suited hands to upper right)

BB	A	K	Q	J	10	9	8	7	6	5	4	3	2
A	C	C	C	C	C	C	C	C	C	C	C	C	C
K	C	C	C	C	C	C	17.8	15.3	14.4	13.3	12.2	11.4	10.8
Q	C	C	C	C	C	16.2	13	10.6	10	8.9	8.5	7.8	7.2
J	C	C	19.9	C	18.4	13.5	10.7	8.8	7.1	6.9	6.2	5.8	5.6
10	C	C	15.6	13.2	C	11.6	9.3	7.4	6.3	5.2	5.2	4.8	4.5
9	C	17.5	11.8	9.9	8.5	C	8.3	7	5.8	5	4.3	4.1	3.9
8	C	14.1	9.8	7.7	6.7	6.1	C	6.5	5.6	4.8	4.1	3.6	3.5
7	C	12.5	8	6.4	5.5	5	4.7	C	5.4	4.8	4.1	3.6	3.3
6	C	11.1	7.4	5.4	4.7	4.2	4.1	4	C	4.9	4.3	3.8	3.3
5	C	10.3	6.8	5.1	4	3.7	3.6	3.6	3.7	C	4.6	4	3.6
4	18.6	9.2	6.3	4.8	3.8	3.3	3.2	3.2	3.3	3.5	C	3.8	3.4
3	16.8	8.8	5.9	4.5	3.6	3.1	2.9	2.9	3	3.1	3	C	3.3
2	16	8.3	5.6	4.2	3.5	3	2.8	2.6	2.7	2.8	2.7	2.6	15.1

[5] Tables reproduced with permission from p136 of *The Mathematics of Poker* by Bill Chen and Jerrod Ankenman, published by ConJelCo © 2006. All rights reserved by the publisher.

Attacker (suited hands to upper right)

SB	A	K	Q	J	10	9	8	7	6	5	4	3	2
A	J	J	J	J	J	J	J	J	J	J	J	J	J
K	J	J	J	J	J	J	J	J	J	J	J	19.9	19.3
Q	J	J	J	J	J	J	J	J	J	J	16.3	13.5	12.7
J	J	J	J	J	J	J	J	J	18.6	16.2	13.5	10.6	8.8
10	J	J	J	J	J	J	J	J	J	11.9	10.5	7.7	6.5
9	J	J	J	J	J	J	J	J	J	14.4	6.9	4.9	3.7
8	J	18.6	13	14.1	18.4	J	J	J	J	18.8	10.1	2.7	2.5
7	J	16.1	10.3	8.5	9.9	10.8	15.6	J	J	J	13.9	2.5	2.1
6	J	15.3	9.8	6.5	5.7	5.2	7.1	11.2	J	J	16.3	*	2
5	J	14.4	8.9	6	4.1	3.5	3	2.6	2.4	J	J	**	2
4	J	13.1	8.3	5.4	3.8	2.7	2.3	2.1	2	2.1	J	***	1.8
3	J	12.5	7.5	5	3.4	2.5	1.9	1.8	1.7	1.8	1.6	J	1.7
2	J	11.6	7	4.6	3	2.2	1.8	1.6	1.5	1.5	1.4	1.4	J

Starred cells indicate hands that have broken strategies:

* 6-3s = 2.3, 5.1-7.1

** 5-3s = 2.4, 4.1-12.9

*** 4-3s = 2.2, 4.8-10

There is little to add to these tables since they provide a stand alone strategy for playing against tough or unknown opponents, but they do offer a very interesting reflection of how far from optimal most player's heads-up strategies are, and reveal much about the comparative values of hands in different situations. For example, with stacks of 15 big blinds or fewer any ace or pair is not only an automatic all-in (which most players understand), but also an automatic call because the wide hand ranges that an optimally playing opponent will shove with means these hands will rarely be dominated even when as marginal as A-2 or 2-2.

Similarly, whilst most players understand the value of suited connectors as all-in hands, these tables also show the extent to which unsuited connectors and suited non-connected cards are undervalued. For example, 8-7 offsuit and J-5 suited are both hands that would be profitable for moving all-in with 15 big blind stacks, simply because (as with suited connectors) you will win the blinds often enough to compensate for the times you are called by a superior hand, and even when that happens you will still have reasonable equity against calling ranges weighted towards high cards and pairs.

A complete explanation of the method used to determine these tables can be found in *The Mathematics of Poker*, where the authors also provide values up to 50 big blinds for all hands. However, for the purposes of this book the maximum values have been restricted to 20 big blinds since you should almost never play an all-in or fold strategy with a stack greater than that, and instead revert to a 'smallball' approach. Note that we have previously talked about the all-in zone as 15 big blinds or less, but when heads-up against tough opposition (or if you are very inexperienced) jamming with hands that will be tough to play postflop like 2-2 or A-2 for as many as 20 big blinds is still acceptable.

You should note, however, that whilst these tables lay out a game theory optimal strategy which will negate any advantage a strong or unknown opponent might have against you, it will be correct to diverge from them against opponents who are much too tight or too loose in order to play an optimal exploitative strategy (i.e. one which is tailored to your opponents weaknesses). For example, against an opponent who only plays very big hands and has not adjusted well to heads-up play you can move all-in with a much wider range than in these tables as you will almost always win the blinds, but you should call an all-in with far fewer hands than they recommend.

Chapter Nine

Strategy for Non-standard Sitngos

Six-max sitngos

Six-max sitngos have become increasingly popular in recent years since they require fewer players to start and allow for more action in the early stages. However, if you are going to play this format you should be more confident in your ability to 'play poker' and make postflop decisions because the blinds will pass through you more frequently and you will not be able to sit back during the early game as much as you would in a full table sitngo. This will be even more true as players are eliminated and the game gets very short-handed, and you will also often reach the bubble with relatively deep stacks compared to a full ring sitngo and need to play postflop at that stage too.

Because of the reduced number of entrants, six-max sitngos usually only pay the top two players with a 65%/35% split between first and second (on some sites this might vary), which will require some strategy adjustments according to ICM. As we have seen, at the 'in the money' stages of a full ring sitngo when three players remain each is guaranteed 20% with the final 40% of the prize pool being divided on a 30%/10%/0% between them, which would be equivalent to a 75%/25%/0% split between the last three players in a six-max sitngo.

However, with a 65%/35%/0% split and second place being more than half of first place, on this standard six-max structure you have a much greater incentive to play for making the money (unless you have a dominating lead) than you would to creep up into second when three-handed in a full ring sitngo. If we consider a six-max $100 sitngo with payouts of $390 for first and $210 for second then with equal stacks on the bubble each player will have a $EV of $200, but if one player doubles through another this alters to:

Player	Stack Size	Tournament Equity ($EV)
Player 1	6000	$330
Player 2	3000	$270
Player 3	0	$0

As we can see, there is significant equity leakage when the bubble bursts in this format since 70% (or $420) of the prize pool is now allocated and the remaining players are only competing for the remaining $180. It is not as serious as on the bubble of a standard sitngo where four players remain and only three get paid, but to play an all-in at this stage you must still be a significant favourite (excluding the presence of blinds and antes):

$$x\% = (\$200/\$330) * 100 = 60.61\%$$

Things get more interesting in this format, however, when there is one big stack and two shorter stacks, since there is now a very big incentive for the short stacks to avoid the bubble. Consider the following scenario:

Player	Stack Size	Tournament Equity ($EV)
Player 1	6000	$316
Player 2	1500	$142
Player 3	1500	$142

Here the big stack is utterly dominant and should be moving all-in almost every hand to exploit the bubble effect (unless the big blind commits a player to calling with a wide range), since even if one of the shorter stacks wins against him their equity is not greatly increased:

Player	Stack Size	Tournament Equity ($EV)
Player 1	4500	$268.50
Player 2	3000	$214
Player 3	1500	$117.50

And, as we can calculate, they will rarely be a sufficient favourite against the big stack's range to warrant this call:

$$x\% = (\$142/\$214) * 100 = 66.36\ \%$$

On the other hand, however, the incentive for each short stack to wait for the other to be eliminated is significant, since when this happens the equity boost they receive is massive. Continuing our example, they would go from a $EV of $142 with two equally short stacks and a big stack to:

Player	Stack Size	Tournament Equity ($EV)
Player 1	7500	$360
Player 2	1500	$240
Player 3	0	$0

What this demonstrates is that, when one player achieves a dominating stack in six-max sitngos, he is in an excellent position to exploit the other two players, who should want to avoid confrontation with him and wait for each other's elimination. Because of this, and because a dominating stack is easier to achieve in a six-max game than in a full ring sitngo, it is often worthwhile to set out with the intention of getting one early in the event where possible, particularly since close gambles at that stage will be less -$EV than in a full ring game where there are three prizes awarded. For example, a player who doubles up early in a six-max sitngo will have slightly more equity than the $184.48 he would in a full ring one:

Player	Stack Size	Tournament Equity ($EV)
Player 1	1500	$103.50
Player 2	1500	$103.50
Player 3	1500	$103.50
Player 4	1500	$103.50
Player 5	3000	$186

Of course, this should not be achieved by looking to take the first all-in opportunity since a coin-flip would still be significantly -$EV here, but by playing a loose-aggressive six-max strategy and being more prepared to play all-in with hands like strong draws than in other instances. This will either lead to you forcing opponents to fold marginal hands and increasing your stack, or to you being all-in and either getting a big stack or being eliminated. If you win then you will be in a good position to work towards bubble domination, and if you lose your equity loss is minimal and will be more than compensated for by the times you make other players fold or get them to put their chips in badly when you have a strong made hand.

Two-table sitngos

With the increase in popularity of sitngos it has become possible for sites to quickly fill games with more than one table, from two-table sitngos right up to ones with 180 players which are effectively multi-table tournaments (apart from not having a designated start time). For the purposes of this book we will not attempt to cover large field events, since these are dealt with in other poker books, but it is worth looking at how the two table format affects your strategy, since these run regularly even at higher stakes.

Two-table sitngos typically consists of 18-20 players and pay four places on a 40%/30%/20%/10% structure. Because only 20% or so of the field will receive prize money, in the early and middle stages you must therefore try to at least double or triple your stack by playing more normal tournament poker in order to stand a chance of making the last four, meaning that you should be more willing to accept thinner edges since the further from the money you are the less equity leakage occurs. However, since this is a much flatter payout structure than other formats and is uniform in that each place above fifth gains a player an additional 10% of the prize pool, once you get close to the money there is far less reason to play for first than in other formats, since even if you creep into second and lose to a massive stack you will still receive 75% of the first-place prize money.

For this reason there is far less incentive to try and achieve a dominating stack in a two-table sitngo than in a six-max one (it would also be considerably harder), and you should be far more averse to taking close gambles in the late stages than even a standard sitngo, since the equity leakage will be massive. For example, with five players left in a 20-player $100 sitngo each has a $EV of $400, but when one doubles through another this only increases by 50%:

Player	Stack Size	Tournament Equity ($EV)
Player 1	12,000	$600
Player 2	6000	$466.67
Player 3	6000	$466.67
Player 4	6000	$466.66

For his play to be +$EV, Player 1 would therefore need to be a massive favourite (excluding the presence of blinds and antes):

$$x\% = (\$400/\$600) * 100 = 66.67\%$$

Correct strategy at this stage therefore consists of a more cautious and patient approach in the hope that other players will be eliminated, allowing you to move up, unless you are in last position already, face the threat of being anted away due to high blinds, or have achieved a dominating stack (in which case you will have now have enormous leverage to use against the other players).

Sitngo satellites (with only one prize)

Sometimes you will see sitngos running that only have one prize, which is usually in the form of entry to a larger event. In such games you are playing a cash game freezeout however many players enter, and you should not think in terms of ICM, since your cEV will always be the same as your $EV. For example, in a 10-player $1000 single table satellite for a $10,000 event, if you start with 1000 chips then each chip will be worth $1 at every stage of the event, until the winner of the satellite has 10,000 chips which are worth $10,000. Because of this you should still play a strategy that accounts for the fact that you cannot rebuy, and you should not gamble recklessly in close situations early on if you are a favourite in the game, but you should usually be prepared to take slightly +cEV opportunities whenever they arise as these will always be +$EV as well.

Sitngo satellites (with more than one prize)

When you are playing a sitngo satellite with more than one prize the structure will be crucial to your strategy. For example, in the example above if the entry fee was $1100 so that second place would get his money back and first would get the $10,000 seat, then you would still mostly want to play to win since your cEV and your $EV would still be similar, although you might now want to avoid very close +cEV gambles since these would now sometimes be -$EV.

However, if you are playing in an event where there are multiple seats to a larger tournament as prizes, then your strategy as the bubble approaches should be more extreme according to ICM than any other we have considered. For example, in a 10-player $80 satellite where four players win entry to a $200 event, with five equally stacked players remaining the situation would look like:

Player	Stack Size	Tournament Equity ($EV)
Player 1	3000	$160
Player 2	3000	$160
Player 3	3000	$160
Player 4	3000	$160
Player 5	3000	$160

If two players were to go all-in here then the equity leakage would be massive, since they would virtually guarantee everyone else a seat in the bigger event. In this example, an all-in player would either gain $40 of equity (by winning a $200 seat) if he won the all-in or lose $160 if he was eliminated, meaning that he would need to be a massive favourite to break even in $EV terms (ignoring any blinds and antes):

$$x\% = (\$160/\$200) * 100 = 80\%$$

Essentially therefore the only hand he would be happy to be all-in with would be aces.

For this reason, playing on the bubble of a satellite offering multiple entries to a larger event is a balancing act between waiting for other players to be eliminated and maintaining a healthy chip stack whilst avoiding all-in confrontations. To succeed you will need to observe closely the stack sizes of all players to see who is in most danger and wait for them to risk elimination before you, whilst also knowing whose blinds you can steal or move all-in against safely and who is likely to call too loosely and risk ruining both your and their own chances.

Making your own assessments of non-standard sitngo structures

As we have seen from considering six-max, two-table sitngos and satellite sitngos, every format requires some alterations in strategy according to the number of players and the payout structure. As there are many sites offering many formats of sitngos, it would be impossible to cover them all, but this book should give you some idea of how to formulate a strategy for them yourself. Such a skill takes time, and in the case of very unusual payout structures like satellites your strategies might need to be altered radically. However, with the application of ICM tools and some basic poker knowledge, most players should be able to adapt well in most structures after reading this book.

When a level is defined by number of hands rather than time

Most sites now run sitngos where the levels are determined in minutes and rise at regular intervals. However, some sites still run ones where the levels are determined by the number of hands played, typically rising every 10 hands or so. In such a format you can easily work out who will face the next blind increase first (assuming that players are not eliminated) and you should use this forward planning to ensure that you are not caught by surprise by a big leap in blinds.

As an aside, when choosing between sitngos with timed levels and those measured by hands played, you should also note that in the latter the length of a level in real time is going to reduce as the sitngo progresses as there will be fewer people to act on each hand. Because of this, unless the blind increases are very smooth you will often find such events quickly turn into crapshoots in the late stages, and for this reason you may prefer to focus on sites where the levels are defined in minutes.

A note on button movement when a player is eliminated

Since the blinds are so big around the bubble stage, you should pay close attention to the rules of the site you are playing on regarding button movement when a player is eliminated. In most poker games when the small blind is eliminated the button should stay in the same position for the next hand since the big blind will now need to pay the small blind, and when the big blind is eliminated it should still move one step on, but there will be no small blind posted in the next hand and only a big blind by the next player, with the button then remaining in that position for the next hand.

This is simply so that no player misses a blind, but some sites (e.g. Poker-Stars) have different rules whereby the button moves one position even when a player in the blinds is eliminated, meaning that someone may miss a blind if they are under-the-gun and one of the blinds is eliminated, or if they are the big blind and the small blind is eliminated. It is important to know what rules the site you are playing on has for these situations, since knowing that the button may jump a player can alter your strategy significantly if it reduces the number of hands you have before having to post the big blind, or if you know that you may miss the big blind if a short stack in the blinds is eliminated when you are under-the-gun.

Chapter Ten

Miscellaneous Topics

The limitations of ICM

Although ICM is by far the best way of analysing sitngo situations, there are still certain limitations to it which make its results slightly inaccurate in some areas, and may lead expert players to make slightly different decisions from those it recommends. We will now consider these, and look at how you should adjust your play in such situations:

1. ICM does not account for players' skill levels

As we have seen, at the beginning of a $100 ten player sitngo, each player's $EV is $100, all things being equal. However, this is rarely going to be the case, since there will invariably be players who have an advantage or a disadvantage in that particular field. This will lead some players' true $EV to be significantly higher or lower than this figure (and in the extreme case of a player who has forgotten to unregister and sits the event out, his $EV would be close to $0).

Therefore in the early stages of a sitngo where there is the opportunity for multi-street play and having a large edge over an opponent, highly skilled players should be more averse to taking very close gambles that are +$EV according to ICM than less skilled ones, since they can rightly assume that they will have the opportunity to take advantage of better opportunities later on.

2. ICM does not account for the positioning of blinds

Imagine that our $100 sitngo from earlier in the book has reached the bubble with four players remaining, each having exactly 2500 chips. What is their current EV in the event? Without considering the blinds it would obviously be correct to answer $250 per player. However, by the bubble stage of a sitngo the blinds are usually very high in relation to the average stack and are therefore anything but irrelevant.

Now consider a scenario in which the blinds in our sitngo have somehow reached 1000/2000, meaning that the big blind has 80% of his stack committed and the small blind 40%. Clearly in this situation the big blind has an enormous disadvantage compared to the rest of the table, since he must play this hand almost all of the time, and the button has an enormous advantage. This would need to be reflected in any accurate $EV assessment (although it is nearly impossible to predict exactly), but it is something that ICM would ignore.

In practice such a situation is rare of course, but it is also true that on the bubble in most sitngos the positioning of the blinds and the order in which the various sized stacks must take them (and when they will increase) is important, since they are usually a significant percentage of the average stack. As we have seen above, the inaccuracy of ICM $EV estimations with high blinds is related to the way in which the $EV of the various stacks is eroded by the blinds moving clockwise, and the extent to which shorter stacks are going to be committed to calling for their whole stack when they are forced to post the big blind.

For this reason ICM results are therefore never a 100% accurate reflection of $EV, and in situations where both you and another player have very small stacks (perhaps 0-5 big blinds) but he must always post before you, you have a significant $EV advantage for obvious reasons. And, as we have seen above, the higher the blinds get in relation to the average stack the less accurate ICM becomes.

What this means in practice, and what inexperienced players or those overly reliant on ICM sometimes fail to understand, is that there is still a significant skill factor present during bubble play in most sitngos, and that expert play at this stage includes not only an understanding of the ramifications of ICM, but also its limitations. For this reason, plays that may seem intuitively right may be wrong according to ICM and vice-versa – and it is up to the expert player to weigh all of the factors (including ICM and the positioning of blinds and stacks) in making a decision.

3. ICM calculators may not properly account for the presence of a 'micro-stack'

The preceding concept dealing with high blinds can be extended further to the presence of a 'micro-stack' during bubble play, which may be defined as a stack that cannot even withstand the next round of blinds and is therefore guaranteed to face an all-in situation and probable elimination in the next few hands.

As we have seen, ICM does not account for the positioning of blinds at the table and so the $EV a micro-stack is assigned is transitory, since it will be forced to risk all of it in the immediate future or when the big blind reaches it. For this reason, most players would argue that to voluntarily risk elimination themselves when a micro-stack is present at the table would require a significantly higher $EV edge than that recommended by an ICM calculator.

4. ICM calculators may underestimate the leverage of a dominating stack

If it may be correct to play more conservatively than ICM dictates on the bubble with a micro-stack present when you have a mid-sized stack, then with a dominating stack (i.e. one which cannot be placed close to elimination by losing an all-in) it is often correct to play much looser than ICM dictates, since many players will be folding in situations where they have a slightly positive $EV edge according to ICM.

By extension, with the presence of a micro-stack it may even be correct to move all-in on almost every hand if you are the chip leader. Doing so will either win you the blinds of players who feel compelled to wait for its elimination or ensure that most of the time when the micro-stack is all-in the outcome will either be you gaining the extra chips by eliminating it, or doubling it up (which is rarely a significant $EV loss anyway due to the dead money in the other player's blinds) and keeping the bubble alive, thereby allowing you to dominate for even longer.

5. ICM calculations do not consider 'future play' issues

As we can see from the above, relying on ICM calculations may present problems based on the fact that they only consider one hand in isolation and do not account for what might happen in future hands or the positioning of the blinds. This is a significant flaw when the blinds are high and you are on the bubble, since it results in ICM overvaluing short-stacks that are in danger of being blinded out and undervaluing medium stacks that are able to outlast them.

For this reason, relying strictly on the recommendations of an ICM calculator when you or other players have less than five big blinds on the bubble is probably suboptimal and players should consider other factors too. However this is a problem that the Sitngo Wizard team has attempted to address by introducing a Future Game Simulation feature on their product, which will help you to understand more accurately the adjustments that should be made in such situations.

6. ICM calculators do not consider the $EV of calling

ICM calculators are designed to assess the $EV of folding compared with that of pushing all-in (or calling all-in) and therefore which is preferable. However, this ignores the possibility of there being situations where open-calling may be preferable to both pushing or folding (for example, if you are the small blind against a loose-passive player in the big blind). Mostly they are irrelevant in high blind play, but it is worth remembering that even in the late stages of sitngos there are more options than all-in or fold.

Other ICM considerations

When using an ICM calculator, there are some other considerations that you should bear in mind before taking the decision that is recommended by it. We will consider some of these now:

1. Hand range estimation errors

Although ICM tools are a very useful in understanding bubble play in sitngos and making correct decisions, they are only as accurate as the information provided about other players' hand ranges, and no-one can claim to get these exactly right all of the time. It is therefore worth carefully considering the accuracy of your hand range assumptions in high-risk sitngo situations where you might be eliminated, and sometimes giving up edges that are theoretically slightly +$EV but may have disastrous consequences if your assumptions prove wrong. This is a matter of judgement, but in low-limit sitngos, where the play is erratic, giving up small theoretically +$EV edges is unlikely to impact your bottom line much since you will likely be presented with many highly +$EV edges in future hands anyway.

2. Variance

Although in most circumstances a +$EV ICM reading represents an immediate real money profit for taking that course of action, you must also consider the effect of the variance of pushing every small $EV edge on your bankroll, productivity and overall emotional and mental state. These points require little illustration and players must find an appropriate balance between them, but it is certainly worth remembering that a very bad run can harm your overall profit margin significantly if it leads to you being forced to drop down in stakes, taking time off or playing worse than normal, and therefore sacrificing some very small +$EV edges in the short-term may lead to greater profit and stability in the long-term for some players.

3. Metagame

Although it is true that taking hands in isolation and performing ICM calculations for them will usually yield accurate enough results to determine the best course of action, it is worth noting that your overall strategy and history with opponents can also be important. For instance, if you move all-in with even the smallest perceived +$EV edge at every opportunity, other players will begin to adjust their hand ranges to this, and some may even over-compensate to the point of making calls that are bad for both of you (particularly in the case of inexperienced players). This will certainly impact on your overall ROI over time, since you will have less fold equity against players who perceive you as extremely aggressive and will need to tighten your ranges accordingly. Therefore metagame considerations are another reason why passing up on some of the smallest edges offered to you may be advisable.

Sitngo tools and resources

Various programs and websites have already been mentioned throughout this book, but there are many others that players may want to investigate to further improve their sitngo game. A few that are often recommended are:

ICM calculators

We have already talked about ICM programs like Sitngo End-game Tools (sngegt.com) and Sitngo Wizard (sngwiz.com) which perform all of the calculations necessary to make correct decisions according to ICM principles. However, it is also useful for players to get a grasp of the components that make up such programs from basic ICM spreadsheets like that found at www.chillin411.com, which simply calculate players' $EVs based on the stack sizes and payouts entered and can help determine strategies for game with non-standard payout structures or multi-table tournaments.

Pokerstove.com

Pokerstove calculates the equity of your hand against inputted hand ranges or against a random hand, and these calculations, along with the principles of ICM spreadsheets and pot-odds calculations, are the main components of sophisticated ICM calculators like SNGEGT or Sitngo Wizard. A more basic version which runs hand vs. hand calculations can be found at www.twodimes.net.

Heads-Up Trainer

Heads-Up Trainer is a program that is included with the SNGEGT package (and is part of the free download) that allows players to play the heads-up 'jam or fold' game against an opponent using a game theory optimal strategy. Combined with use of Bill Chen and Jerrod Ankenman's 'jam or fold' tables on pages 101/2 it is an excellent tool for learning game theory optimal heads-up high blind strategy.

SNG quiz generators

Both SNGEGT and Sitngo Wiz contain programs that will generate endless bubble situations until you have the finer points of ICM strategy memorized.

Twoplustwo.com

Twoplustwo is the biggest online public poker forum and community, and includes an active sitngo forum with much educational information and large numbers of players posting and analysing each other's hands.

CardRunners.com

CardRunners is an online poker training site providing daily videos of professionals playing and analysing games. They cover all poker games and formats and instructors include legendary hi-stakes cash game players Brian Townsend, Taylor Caby and Cole South, as well as the author of this book, who is an instructor on sitngos under the name 'Jackal'. In addition to the videos there is also a members only forum providing additional advice and discussion between pros and members.

Bankroll, ROI and variance

A poker bankroll, in simple terms, is an amount of money stored up to play with that should be sufficient to withstand the short-term fluctuations of the game and reduce the probability that you ever 'go broke' to almost zero. Calculating an adequate bankroll for playing sitngos (which should be expressed as a number of buy-ins) is therefore a function of a player's ROI (return on investment), their willingness to accept risk, and whether or not it is going to be depleted for expenses or other reasons along the way.

This means that, although there are some general guidelines you should follow, bankroll is to some extent a personal consideration. For example, consider two strong middle-stakes players with a 10% ROI, one of whom is a parentally-supported college student with the prospect of a promising career, whilst the other is a much older poker professional with a family, mortgage, car and so on.

Even though their skill levels are the same, the student will probably be happier to take more risks and play with a smaller bankroll, since the consequences of going broke are less severe and he can rebuild if things go wrong or continue in his career path. Whereas the older player should be highly risk-averse since the consequences of going broke, or even having to drop down in stakes, would be disastrous. Also, with fewer overheads and a smaller required bankroll, the student is likely to move up in stakes quicker than the pro, since his bankroll is not depleted as often and he can afford to take a more aggressive approach to increasing the stakes he plays for, with the potential of greater future profit.

These are two extreme cases, and the reality is that most players fall somewhere inbetween. However, it is also the case that most sitngo players (and poker players in general) drastically underestimate what an adequate bankroll is, and even those that do know often ignore it. It is therefore advisable that you follow some general guidelines so that, if you do decide to throw caution to the wind, at least you will know that you are taking an increased risk and be prepared for the consequences, whether positive or negative.

We have already said that bankroll calculations should be based on an acceptable theoretical risk of ruin, ROI and depletion considerations, so we need to set parameters for these. Let's say that the model player is prepared to accept a 5% or less theoretical risk of ruin at a fixed buy-in level (of course you should never actually 'go broke' if you are prepared to drop down in stakes at an appropriate time), and that he is prepared to keep his bankroll separate from other monies and not deplete it. Now we must consider what an achievable ROI is for players at certain stakes. From looking at databases of high volume players and through general consensus, we can assume the following maximum ROIs for the best players at given levels over large numbers of games:

Below $100 (Low stakes): 15% ROI

At this level there will be many bad players with little or no idea of how to play either poker in general or sitngos in particular, and the ratio of serious to recreational players will be low. For this reason a 15% ROI should be achievable for players with some basic poker knowledge who have also studied sitngo strategy, and it should be maintainable as their skill level will rapidly increase as they move up in stakes.

$100-$499 (Mid-stakes): 10% ROI

As players break the $100 buy-in mark they will start to encounter many more skilled players and the ratio of serious to recreational players will be significantly worse than at the low stakes games. However there will still be many average and bad players around, and players will also get a boost in ROI from the entry fees beginning to drop from 10% (e.g. $100+$9, $200+$15 and $300+$20). For this reason the best players should still be able to achieve a ROI of 10% with a little game selection, and show a healthy profit.

$500 and above (High stakes): 5% ROI

At the highest stakes sitngos (which currently go up to $5000) there will be many highly skilled players, including some of the best sitngo players in the world, and few weaker players in proportion to them. For this reason game selection will become an important issue, and selecting sitngos where there are more rich recreational players, or playing at off-peak hours, where the best players are elsewhere, will be very beneficial for all but the best. At these levels the entry fee will have dropped to only 5% of the buy-in, but because of the sudden switch in ratios of good to bad players it will be very hard for players to achieve more than a 5% ROI over a large sample size.

With these assumptions and some statistical analysis we can therefore set the following general bankroll guidelines, based on your estimated ROI:

15% ROI – 40 buy-ins or more

10% ROI – 60 buy-ins or more

5% ROI –100 buy-ins or more

These numbers of buy-ins should be adequate for players who want to be able to play comfortably at any given level, but it is important to also consider the actual real life situations and bankroll issues that players will face. For example, these numbers assume that a player will never move up or down in stakes, whilst in reality most players aspire to play in bigger games and make more money, and some lose enough of their bankrolls that they are forced to step down a level.

With these bankroll guidelines the latter should rarely be case, since they are based on the idea that a player will add all profits to their initial bankroll and should rarely have a significant enough downswing overall that they should have to move down in stakes. For example, if we assume that every buy-in level for a certain site is either double or half the ones either side of it (e.g. $5, $10, $20 etc), then it would be reasonable for a player with 40 buy-ins at a certain level and a 15% ROI to admit defeat and move down if he lost half his bankroll, since he would still then have 40 buy-ins at the level below and face little risk of ruin there.

Now a player with a 15% ROI in these games will be lucky to not experience a 20 buy-in downswing at some point in their time playing small stakes sitngos, but unless they lose from the outset at this level and drop from 40 to 20 buy-ins without increasing their bankroll at any point they will usually be able to withstand the subsequent swings, and only rarely be forced to move down. Similarly, 60 and 100 buy-in bankrolls for players with 10% and 5% ROIs will allow them to withstand 30 and even 50 buy-in downswings respectively without usually having to move down in stakes.

It should be noted, however, that a 20 buy-in downswing with a 15% ROI is still far more likely to occur than a 50 buy-in one with a 5% ROI, simply because of the variance inherent in sitngos. However, players with a 40 buy-in bankroll and 15% ROI will withstand such downswings with greater ease, since they will increase their initial bankroll at a far higher rate proportionally than those at with 100 buy-ins and a 5% ROI, and therefore usually have a larger cushion to fall back on.

You should also note that large downswings are not uncommon for players in very high stakes games or with very low ROIs, and that you should be prepared for occasional downswings whatever stakes you play, both in terms of having an adequate bankroll and psychologically by being prepared to take time off and avoid tilting, which will lower your ROI even further. However, by following these guidelines you should still experience far more stability in the stakes that you can play than others with more risk taking approaches, which will in turn add to your overall profitability.

Moving up!

We have talked about the worst-case scenario, where things go badly and you may be in danger of having to drop down in stakes. However, for most winning players this will rarely be the case, and you will mostly need to consider how to move up in stakes most efficiently. Since there is no maximum bankroll for a given limit, there are fewer rigid rules on how this should be approached (assuming of course that players do not put the bankroll for their current stakes in jeopardy when trying to move up).

Therefore a player with 40 buy-ins for $10 sitngos (i.e. $400) and a 15% ROI may simply keep playing them till his bankroll reaches $800 and he has 40 buy-ins to start playing $20 sitngos with, or he may choose to 'take shots' at the next level with any surplus funds available beyond the $400 required to keep playing at the $10 level, particularly if he sees some weak games about to start. What approach players take is really up to them, providing they practise sensible bankroll management overall and again individual risk/reward considerations are important.

For example, a player at the $10 level who waits patiently until he has 40 buy-ins for the $20 level is very unlikely to even have to drop below the $10 level, since he will always have some cushioning from the additional buy-ins he has stored up if a downswing occurs. So, if he increases his initial $400 bankroll to $700 and has a 20 buy-in downswing of $200 he will still have $500, which is more than enough to continue playing $10 sitngos with. However, if a player at the $10 level with a $400 bankroll chooses to use every additional $20 he makes beyond that amount to take shots at the $20 sitngos and is not successful, a subsequent 20 buy-in downswing at the $10 games would put him in danger of having to drop down to the $5 games.

On the other hand, however, a player who waits patiently to have 40 buy-ins at the next level may pass up highly +$EV shot-taking opportunities that could have got him there much faster, and a player aggressively taking shots may therefore move up the levels much quicker than his more conservative counterpart. For this reason, a mixed strategy between these two extremes focusing on 'intelligent shot taking' is probably the best overall approach, although exactly what is best for each player and how to manage moving up is for them to determine.

It should also be noted that as players move up in stakes, the number of games running, and the number of good games within that number, will reduce to the point where players are not able to find enough games at one particular level to keep them at full capacity. For this reason, most higher stakes players tend to play a mixture of games within certain parameters, and bankroll can therefore be calculated by using an average. For example:

Level	Distribution of Buy-ins	Average Buy-in
Mid-stakes	$200 (50%), $300 (50%)	$250
Hi stakes	$500 (40%), $1000 (40%), $2000 (20%)	$1000

From $200 to $100,000 in one year (and 5000 sitngos)

Having made some assumptions and calculations about how the model sitngo player might approach bankroll management and moving up in stakes, we can now start to look at the 'career' of a sitngo player and how long he might realistically take to progress from $5 sitngos to the highest limits (and how much money he would make along the way).

For the sake of simplicity we will assume the conditions already set out above regarding ROI and bankroll at certain buy-in levels and that the round numbers used for each include entry fees, so a $10 sitngo might be $9+$1, with a player's ROI being $1.50 (players can construct their own tables based on what site they play and their ROI). Of course, ROI as a percentage should decrease more incrementally than suggested below at each individual buy-in level, but sudden drops in ROI (and possibly even temporary drops in overall ROI) will still be experienced by players trying to move up as they cross certain thresholds and start to encounter players who play predominately mid- or high stakes games. Therefore, they do in this sense mirror the real experiences of sitngo players trying to move up.

We will also assume our model player will not take shots and will win uniformly according to his ROI, simply moving up as and when he has an adequate bankroll for the next level. Of course, few players progress will be as smooth or risk- averse as this, but as we have seen this player would rarely have to drop down in stakes with such a strategy. Finally, since there are many more buy-in levels available at the lower stakes games that the higher stakes ones, this should also be reflected.

Using all of these assumptions we can predict our player's progress, which would look like the following assuming he started at the $5 level with a bankroll of $200 and moved up as recommended above until he reached $100,000 and could afford to play games with an average buy-in of $1000. At each level his ROI and initial bankroll are recorded, along with the number of games he will need to play before moving to the next level:

Stakes	Level	ROI($)	Initial Bankroll	Sitngos to move up
	$5	$0.75	$200	267
	$10	$1.50	$400	267
LOW	$20	$3	$800	133
	$30	$4.50	$1200	178
	$50	$7.50	$2000	533
	$100	$10	$6000	600
MID	$200	$20	$12,000	300
	$300	$30	$18,000	1067
HIGH	$500*	$30	$50,000	1667
	$1000*	$50	$100,000	
	Total			5012

* Note that these are average buy-in figures and that with an average buy-in of $500 we have assumed a 6% ROI to account for playing some mid-stakes games.

As we can see therefore, a player who consistently moves up and improves to ensure that he keeps achieving the maximum possible ROI at that level can expect to go from $5 games to those with an average buy-in of $1000 in a little over 5000 games, assuming he never depletes his bankroll. At this stage he will have increased his bankroll from $200 to $100,000, a seemingly outlandish achievement, but one that is certainly achievable for players who are dedicated, capable and willing to study away from the tables.

Assuming that our model player is all of these things, how long might this journey take? Well, 5012 sitngos would be almost 14 games a day for a year, which multi-tabling 4-6 at a time might translate to 2-3 hours of actual play per day, or 15-20 hours a week (with some additional study time needed). Although this is a serious time commitment, it could still be done in one year as a 'part-time job' by most students, or over a longer period by those with more commitments (or who decide to cash out along the way). However, even a studious recreational player with a full-time job should be able to progress from the $5 to the $100 games in a year, since this would require only 26.5 games and 6-8 hours play a week.

As we can see, however, it is those that aim to progress to the highest levels who will need to put in the most hours, since at middle and high stakes sitngos the bankroll needed is larger and the ROI is smaller, with players at the $300 level needing to play on average over 1000 games there to build a bankroll for the $500 games and then 1667 more in order to play at the highest stakes regularly available. However, the rewards for those getting there will be rich indeed, since they will now be making an average of $50 per sitngo and will only need to play 2000 games in the next year to make the same $100,000 that it took over 5000 games to achieve initially.

Such figures will certainly seem outlandish to many readers, and many will never reach these heights (or take longer to do so) for any number of reasons. However, the fact remains that some players will certainly make such leaps in the coming years, and that many of the big names of online poker today (such as Taylor Caby and Phil Galfold) built their bankrolls playing sitngos and went far beyond, expanding them into seven figure fortunes in high stakes cash games. The important thing to remember is that most players are at least capable of rising to and winning in mid-high stakes sitngos, and that the question is almost always one of choice and dedication.

Rakeback

One subject that is very important for sitngo players is rakeback, which means the percentage of rake generated that poker sites are willing to give back to their players as bonuses or rewards. Each site offers a different percentage, and some have VIP schemes instead where rewards are determined by your volume of play such as PokerStars, but wherever you play rakeback will be essential if you are going to maximise your profit as a sitngo player.

For example, on Full Tilt Poker you can get 27% rakeback, so for every $1 you pay in tournament fees you will receive back 27 cents. Therefore if you are a beginning player playing 100 $11 + 1 games per month you will rake $100 and get back $27 in that period, or $324 per year. If you are a professional high stakes player however you might play 500 games a month with an average fee of $20, meaning an enormous $2,700 in rakeback per month or $32,400 per year.

Given that your overall return on investment might be 10% in a low-mid stakes game or 5% in a high stakes game, rakeback will therefore make up a significant proportion of this figure. So in a $11+1 game a 10% ROI would be $1.20, of which 27 cents or 22.5% might be rakeback, and without it you would be making only 93 cents per game for a 7.75% ROI. Similarly, in a $300+20 game a 5% ROI would be $16 of which $5.40 or 33.75% would be rakeback, and without which your actual ROI would drop to 3.3125%.

Clearly therefore, the higher in stakes you play the more important rakeback becomes. This is also increasingly the case as the average standard of play in sitngos improves over time, which can even allow players who would not be profitable without rakeback to still make a small profit with it. However, whatever level you play at you should only do so with rakeback since it is essentially free money, and you can sign up for it at http://rakeupdate.com/signup/secretsofsitngos by opening a new poker site account through one of the links with the relevant bonus code, then entering your account information in the adjacent boxes so that you can be identified by the rakeback administrators.

You will then be signed up and be able to login to the members section using the details sent to your email account, where you can check how much rakeback you have accumulated. This figure is updated daily, and cashouts are normally processed within 24 hours and can be accessed by clicking the link below your balance and choosing from a variety of sites for payment including Neteller, Money Bookers, Full Tilt Poker and Cake Poker.

Rakeback rates vary between sites depending on their size and reputation, with Full Tilt Poker offering 27%; Bodog, Absolute Poker, Ultimate Bet, PKR, Eurolinx, Aced, NQIQ, InterPoker and Betfair offering 30% and Cake Poker offering 33%. Sites will also offer 'first deposit bonuses' based on these criteria, which will be gradually paid as you accumulate rake. For example, Full Tilt Poker offers a '100% match bonus up to $600', meaning that if you deposit an amount of $600 or below you get that much in bonuses allocated to your account to earn through playing there, and on smaller sites you may even get bonus offers of greater than 100% or for amounts up to $1500. Wherever you play however, always check the terms and conditions to see how much you need to play and in what period to claim back this amount since, unlike rakeback which is fixed, the small print can vary significantly between sites.

In terms of choosing where you should play, the biggest sites for sitngos are Full Tilt Poker, PokerStars, and Cake Poker, although you may find weaker opposition on smaller sites like PRK, Betfair, Bodog and Interpoker (though there will also be less action). You may also sign up for Absolute Poker and Ultimate Bet at the above link, but players should be more cautious about playing at these sites because of a history of problems with game integrity, security and management. Players should therefore experiment with different sites to find ones which suit them best in terms of standard of opposition, rakeback deals, frequency of games, security and customer service.

Wherever you play however, if you are hoping to make serious money out of sitngos, or even plan on just playing a few a week, remember that rakeback will be an essential way of maximising your profit, and that the more you play the more you will earn. Therefore if you intend to open a new account at a poker site simply go to http://rakeupdate.com/signup/secretsofsitngos first and sign up there, and you will be able to save yourselves hundreds or even thousands of dollars over the course of your sitngo career.

The future of sitngos

It is undoubtedly the case that since sitngos first became popular, the general standard of play has improved greatly (as it has in cash games and multi-table tournaments), and that ICM calculators and other programs have advanced the understanding of correct strategy significantly. However, this is not to say that sitngos have become less profitable, or that in the future everyone is likely to be playing a perfect strategy, making them obsolete as a way of making money.

This is because there will always be players who are more advanced than others, and have devoted more time to studying correct strategies, thinking about different situations, and putting in the hours at the tables. At one end of the scale will be professionals or semi-professionals putting in large numbers of games and making substantial profits, and at the other will be recreational players coming to the games as poker continues to gain popularity worldwide. Many of the latter will either take up sitngos immediately or find their way to them after trying cash games and multi-table tournaments, since they prefer the convenience and simplicity of the format, the reduced edge that the best players have over them, and that they can regularly make the money positions.

In addition to them new players (many of whom will be studious and read books like this) will continue to get their start in poker through sitngos since they are an excellent way to build a bankroll and develop an understanding of poker concepts without having to deal with too many complicated situations in the early days of their careers. These players will work their way up the ranks to become the high limit players of tomorrow, and many will make good money from the game whether they play it in their spare time, as semi-pros or fully-fledged professionals.

All of these groups of players will continue to ensure that the sitngo economy stays healthy for many years to come, and as cash games start to dry up because the best players win too easily, and players become frustrated with the variance and time commitments associated with multi-table tournaments, they may even gain popularity in relative terms. Whichever group of players you fall into, however, the most likely reason that sitngos will continue to be popular is the one that first drew you to them through the thrill of the all-in confrontation, the relief of making the money, and the pleasure of winning again – sitngos are fun!

Chapter Eleven

Sitngo Quizzes

Introducing the quiz section

The following hand examples are designed to illustrate key concepts in the main text, but are presented as real world scenarios with multiple choice questions followed by answers for players to judge their own decision-making abilities. They follow the sections as set out in the main text, so readers may wish to refer back as they go or reread sections that they feel they are struggling with conceptually while working through them.

The early game

1. Playing a small pair in early position

Game:	$11 9-player turbo sitngo
Players left:	9
Hand:	3♦-3♥
Position:	UTG
Blinds:	10/20
Stacks:	

UTG	+1	+2	+3	+4	CO	Button	SB	BB
1500	1500	1500	1500	1500	1500	1500	1500	1500
YOU								

Action

It is the first hand of an $11 sitngo and you know nothing about the other players, but assume that they will be quite weak at this level. You are dealt 3-3 under-the-gun. Do you a) fold, b) call c) raise to 60 or d) go all-in?

Answer

b) call. Although you do not yet know what type of game you are in, a small pocket pair will usually be profitable here and by limping you maximise your chances of seeing a cheap flop. At higher stakes you might fold, as the typical game type would be tight-aggressive, but at this level you can expect to be against looser players who might double you up if you flop a set. Remember not to take this idea too far, however, as limping with hands like Q-Jo or 7-4s would be unlikely to show a profit even here.

2. Playing suited connectors in late position

Game: $22 9-player turbo sitngo

Players left: 9

Hand: 7♦-6♦

Position: Button

Blinds: 15/30

Stacks:

UTG	+1	+2	+3	+4	CO	Button	SB	BB
1500	1500	1500	1500	1500	1500	1500	1500	1500
						YOU		

Action

It is the first hand of a $20 sitngo where the blinds start at 15/30. You are on the button with 7-6s and there are four limpers before you. Do you a) fold, b) call c) raise to 150 or d) go all-in?

Answer

c) call. This is the perfect time to call with a suited connector in the early game as you have position and there are several limpers already, meaning that even with 50 big blind stacks this will be profitable.

3. Playing a strong hand in early position

Game: $50 9-player standard speed sitngo

Players left: 9

Hand: A♦-Q♦

Position: UTG+1

Blinds: 10/20

Stacks:

UTG	+1	+2	+3	+4	CO	Button	SB	BB
1500	1500	1530	1520	1530	1500	1470	1470	1480
	YOU							

Action

Early on in a tight-aggressive $50 standard speed sitngo you are dealt A-Qs in early position and the UTG player folds. Do you a) fold, b) call, c) raise to 60 or d) move all-in?

Answer

c) raise to 60. This is a premium hand in any position and you should raise for value and to limit the field. Because this is a tight game raising to 60 is fine, but in a looser one you may want to make it 80. Note that because this is a standard speed game and you will have longer to find good hands, you may want to fold slightly worse hands than this like A-10o in early position, since you will rarely get called by worse hands and may end up trapping yourself.

4. Playing a strong hand against limpers

Game: $50 9-player standard speed sitngo

Players left: 9

Hand: A♦-Q♦

Position: Cut-off

Blinds: 10/20

Stacks:

UTG	+1	+2	+3	+4	CO	Button	SB	BB
1500	1500	1530	1520	1530	1500	1470	1470	1480
					YOU			

Action

In the same game as above you are again dealt A-Qs, but this time you are the cut-off and there are two limpers in early position. Do you a) fold, b) call, c) raise to 100 or d) raise all-in?

Answer

c) raise to 100. You have a very strong hand and position against players who have shown no strength so far, so you should make an isolation raise to knock out the blinds and force the limpers to either fold or call and play a bigger pot out of position. Note that whereas in a cash game you might isolation raise with many hands here (particularly against weaker players), in a sitngo with shallow stacks you should be more interested in calling and playing smallball unless you have a premium hand.

5. Playing suited Broadway in late position

Game: $105 9-player turbo sitngo

Players left: 8

Hand: Q♠-10♠

Position: Button

Blinds: 10/20

Stacks:

UTG	+1	+2	+3	CO	Button	SB	BB
1500	3030	1530	1520	1500	1470	1470	1480
					YOU		

Action

Everyone folds to you in on the button in a $105 turbo and you have Q-10s against the blinds who are tight-aggressive players. Do you a) fold, b) call, c) raise to 60 or d) go all-in?

Answer

c) raise to 60. This is a very playable hand in late position. You are unlikely to be reraised by the blinds and even if they call you still have position. Beware, however, of opening such hands in early position or raising with low suited connectors in mid-position, and try to adjust your ranges slightly to how the blinds play.

6. Facing a reraise

Game: $15 9-player turbo sitngo

Players left: 7

Hand: A♠-J♣

Position: UTG+2

Blinds: 10/20

Stacks:

UTG	+1	+2	CO	Button	SB	BB
3200	3030	1470	1500	1320	1480	1500
		YOU				

Action

Early on in a loose-aggressive $15 turbo in which two players have already been eliminated you raise to 80 in mid-position with A-Jo and are reraised by the small blind, who has not yet played a hand, to 320. Do you a) fold, b) call or c) raise all-in?

Answer

a) fold. Although this appears to be a wild low-limit game, you are up against a player who has made a big raise against you out of position on the first hand he has entered. Give him credit for a strong hand and adjust your ranges in future if he proves to be a maniac.

7. Facing a raise with A-K

Game: $215 9-player turbo sitngo

Players left: 9

Hand: A♠-K♣

Position: Cut-off

Blinds: 10/20

Stacks:

UTG	+1	+2	+3	+4	CO	Button	SB	BB
1500	1500	1530	1520	1530	1500	1470	1470	1480
					YOU			

Action

On the first hand of a $215 turbo sitngo a mid-position raiser who you know as a tight-aggressive regular makes it 60 after everyone folds. You have A-Ko in the cut-off. Do you a) fold, b) call, c) raise to 200 or d) move all-in?

Answer

c) raise to 200. Your hand is far ahead of his range so you should reraise to gain value and force him to fold weaker hands, and also reraise with other hands like A-Q and 10-10+. If the raise came from early position, you might elect to just call sometimes, and only reraise with hands like A-Ks, Q-Q+.

8. Facing an all-in with A-K

Game: $215 9-player turbo sitngo

Players left: 9

Hand: A♠-K♣

Position: Cut-off

Blinds: 10/20

Stacks:

UTG	+1	+2	+3	+4	CO	Button	SB	BB
1500	1500	1530	1520	1530	1500	1470	1470	1480
					YOU			

Action

In the same hand as above the tight-aggressive regular now goes all-in for 1500, making it 1300 to call for you to win 1730. Do you a) fold or b) call?

Answer

a) fold. As we saw in 'the early game' section, you would have to believe your opponents range included A-Q for you to call here, and it is unlikely that a tight-aggressive player would make such a play with that hand here. Against a range of Q-Q+, A-K you only have about 40% equity and so based on pot odds alone you should fold.

9. Facing a reraise with A-K

Game: $55 9-player turbo sitngo

Players left: 9

Hand: A♠-K♣

Position: UTG+4

Blinds: 10/20

Stacks:

UTG	+1	+2	+3	+4	CO	Button	SB	BB
1460	1450	1500	1500	1500	1550	1510	1560	1470
				YOU				

Action

In a $55 turbo you open to 80 in mid-position with A-Ko and a loose-aggressive player in the big blind reraises to 260. Do you a) fold, b) call or c) move all-in?

Answer

c) move all-in. Here the crucial difference from the previous hand is that you are able to move all-in with A-K rather than having to call all-in with it, although other factors like your position and the type of player you are up against are in your favour too. You should make this play against all but the tightest players, or when you have raised in early position and been reraised by a solid player, in which case calling a standard sized reraise and taking a flop might sometimes be preferable.

10. Facing a raise in the big blind

Game: $320 9-player turbo sitngo

Players left: 9

Hand: A♦-8♥

Position: Big Blind

Blinds: 10/20

Stacks:

UTG	+1	+2	+3	+4	CO	Button	SB	BB
1400	1500	1530	1470	1500	1600	1500	1500	1500
								YOU

Action

In a $320 turbo sitngo you are in the big blind and face a raise to 80 from a loose-aggressive late-position raiser. You have A-8o. Do you a) fold, b) call, c) raise to 280 or d) move all-in?

Answer

a) fold. Although you are against a loose player you are out of position with a marginal hand and will lose money overall if you call here, since you will usually miss the flop and may have kicker trouble if you do catch an ace. Hands like A-J, A-10 and small pocket pairs are playable here for at least a call, and you should certainly reraise in this situation with A-Q+, 10-10+. If the small blind makes the opening raise, however, you will have position and so will be able to defend with marginal hands more often, although you should still proceed cautiously if they are very tight players.

11. Getting good pot odds in the small blind

Game: $100 9-player standard speed sitngo

Players left: 9

Hand: K♠-6♦

Position: Small Blind

Blinds: 10/20

Stacks:

UTG	+1	+2	+3	+4	CO	Button	SB	BB
1500	1500	1500	1500	1500	1500	1500	1500	1500
							YOU	

Action

On the first hand of a $100 standard speed sitngo you are dealt K-6o in the small blind and there are four limpers. Do you a) fold, b) call, c) raise to 120 or d) move all-in?

Action

a) fold. Although you are getting excellent pot odds, this hand will be very hard to play profitably after the flop unless you make two pair or better, as even when you flop a king you may face kicker problems, and so you should think more about reverse implied odds here. Hands that you can complete with after limpers in addition to those already discussed in other limping situations include ones like J-10o, Q-10o, Q-9s and 8-6s, which although borderline will not get you into as much trouble and have good implied odds. You may also want to limp with hands like these when all players fold to you in the small blind and the big blind is passive.

12. Playing A-K with a deeper stack

Game: $111 9-player standard sitngo

Players left: 8

Hand: A♣-K♠

Position: Cut-off

Blinds: 15/30

Stacks:

UTG	+1	+2	+3	CO	Button	SB	BB
2000	1540	1200	1500	2600	1500	1560	1600
				YOU			

Action

In a $55 turbo where one player has already been eliminated you have A-Ko in the cut-off. Two players fold and the next player with 1200 chips raises to 90, so you reraise to 300, then he pushes all-in for 1200. It is 900 to you to win 1545. Do you a) fold or b) call?

Answer

b) call. The improved pot odds from the rise in blinds and your opponent's shorter stack combined with your extra chips make this a call. If you fold your $EV will be $163.35, but if you call it will increase to $248.21 if you win and decrease to $106.34 if you lose, so you only need to be have 40.18% or better equity here. Even against an all-in range of AQ+, TT+ you have 49.18% equity, which would make this an easy call.

13. Playing a shorter stack

Game: $215 10-player turbo sitngo

Players left: 10

Hand: 8♥-8♠

Position: Small Blind

Blinds: 15/30

Stacks:

UTG	+1	+2	+3	+4	+5	CO	Button	SB	BB
1500	1500	1520	1500	1560	1420	1500	1500	750	2250
								YOU	

Action

In a $215 turbo you have lost half of your stack early on and now have 8-8 on the small blind with 750 chips. A mid-position raiser makes it 90 and the cut-off calls. Do you a) fold, b) call, c) raise to 300 or d) move all-in?

Answer

d) move all-in. There are already 225 chips in the pot to win and you do not want to see a flop with 8-8 as it will be difficult to play unless you hit a set, but it is too strong to fold. By using your stack like this you can force the other players to a tough decision, boosting your chips by over 30% when they fold and still being in a coin-flip against A-K or A-Q some of the time when you are called.

14. Playing postflop when you have been called and missed

Game: $50 9-player standard sitngo

Players left: 9

Hand: Q♠-J♣

Position: Button

Blinds: 10/20

Stacks:

UTG	+1	+2	+3	+4	CO	Button	SB	BB
1500	1500	1500	1500	1500	1500	1500	1500	1500
						YOU		

Action

It is the first hand of a $50 standard speed sitngo, and everyone folds to you on the button, so you raise to 60 with Q-Jo. The big blind calls and checks a flop of K♠-8♦-2♥ to you. Do you a) check, b) bet 80 or c) move all-in?

Answer

b) bet 80. Although this looks like a bad flop for you it is also unlikely to have hit your opponent and therefore you will often win with a continuation bet of 2/3 to 3/4 of the pot. If you are called or raised, however, you should not usually put any more chips in the pot.

15. Playing a monster hand postflop

Game:	$20 9-player sitngo
Players left:	9
Hand:	3♦-3♥
Position:	Button
Blinds:	10/20
Stacks:	

UTG	+1	+2	+3	+4	CO	Button	SB	BB
1500	1500	1500	1500	1500	1500	1500	1500	1500
						YOU		

Action

On the first hand of a $20 9-player sitngo against unfamiliar opposition the UTG player raises to 60 and is called by two players, so with excellent odds and position you also call with 3♦-3♥ on the button. The flop comes 3♠-8♣-K♦ and the opener bets 180 into the 270 pot, getting called by one player with the other folding. There is now 570 in the pot and you have 1440 behind. Do you a) fold, b) call, c) raise to 540 or d) move all-in?

Answer

c) call. On a draw heavy board like 3♠-10♠-J♣ you would want to raise on the flop to protect your hand and get more chips in the pot, but here you should just call in position and wait for the turn to spring your trap, or even the river if it looks like that will be the best way of maximising your equity and no scare card comes on the turn. In a sitngo trips is always a monster and should be played for all your chips unless the board is very scary. Two pair is of similar strength (though slightly weaker) and should be played the same way, unless it is a low two pair and multiple players are all-in on a dry board.

16. Playing top pair, high kicker postflop

Game:	$78 9-player turbo sitngo
Players left:	9
Hand:	A♦-Q♦
Position:	UTG+3
Blinds:	15/30
Stacks:	

UTG	+1	+2	+3	+4	CO	Button	SB	BB
1550	1520	1430	1500	1500	1515	1500	1485	1500
			YOU					

Action

Early on in a $78 turbo you open in mid-position to 60 with A-Qs. The big blind, who is a semi-loose aggressive regular, calls and checks the flop of A♥-10♠-7♠ to you, so you bet 180 for value. He calls and checks the turn which is the 2♣, and there is now 545 in the pot with you having 1330 behind. Do you a) check, b) bet 250, c) bet 420 or d) move all-in?

Answer

c) bet 420. At this stage it is unlikely you have the worst hand as most aggressive players would usually have checkraised a draw-laden flop like that out of position with a strong hand. Therefore your opponent likely has a worse ace than you (as he would usually reraise A-K preflop) or a draw, and so you should make a sizeable bet but one that still allows him to make an incorrect call or believe that you might fold if he reraises all-in.

17. Facing river aggression with top pair, high kicker

Game: $78 9-player turbo sitngo

Players left: 9

Hand: A♦-Q♦

Position: UTG+3

Blinds: 15/30

Stacks:

UTG	+1	+2	+3	+4	CO	Button	SB	BB
1550	1520	1430	1500	1500	1515	1500	1485	1500
			YOU					

Action

Continuing the above hand, you bet 420 on the turn and the big blind calls again. The river comes the J♠ making the board A♥-10♠-7♠-2♣-J♠ and now he moves all-in for 910 first to act, which you must call to win 2105. Do you a) fold or b) call?

Answer

a) fold. The J♠ completes every conceivable draw and also gives A-J two pair. Your opponent has shown no aggression until this point and you will need to win over 30.18% of the time to show a profit, but the only hand you can really beat here is a bluff and he is unlikely to show up with that so often.

18. Playing a strong draw

Game:	$10 turbo 9-player sitngo
Players left:	9
Hand:	9♥-8♥
Position:	Cut-off
Blinds:	10/20
Stacks:	

UTG	+1	+2	+3	+4	CO	Button	SB	BB
1460	1470	1500	1580	1520	1500	1500	1500	1470
					YOU			

Action

In a $10 turbo you are in the cut-off with 9♥-8♥ at a table you expect to be quite loose and passive from previous experience with some of the players. Three players limp in front of you and you limp on the cut-off after which the button folds, the small blind completes and the big blind checks. The flop comes 6♥-7♣-A♥ and the big blind bets 100 into the pot of 120, with two of the loose limpers calling, taking the pot to 420. Do you a) fold, b) call, c) raise to 400 or d) move all-in?

Answer

b) call. Although you have flopped a massive draw that would not be in trouble against many hands all-in you should still usually err on the side of caution in a sitngo rather than play for a high risk double up, especially against loose-passive players. Calling is especially good here since you have excellent position and pot odds, and will be able to make the most of hitting your hand on the turn and maybe even get to see a cheap river card if you miss there.

19. Playing a weaker draw

Game: $10 turbo 9-player sitngo

Players left: 9

Hand: 9♥-8♥

Position: Cut-off

Blinds: 10/20

Stacks:

UTG	+1	+2	+3	+4	CO	Button	SB	BB
1460	1470	1500	1580	1520	1500	1500	1500	1470
					YOU			

Action

The situation is the same as the above hand, however this time the flop has come 6♠-7♠-A♠. The big blind bets 100 into the 120 pot and two players call. Do you a) fold, b) call, c) raise to 420 or d) move all-in?

Answer

a) fold. Here your draw is considerably weaker, as with three spades out you may already be drawing dead to a flush and even if this is not the case you will still only have six straight cards to hit as another spade will usually make someone a flush. The latter would also be true if there were only two spades on the flop and someone else had a flush draw, although you may then still call in such a situation at a weak table getting good pot odds with six clean outs. Here though calling would be a disaster and it is a clear fold.

20. Playing a strong combo-draw

Game: $525 turbo 9-player sitngo

Players left: 9

Hand: J♠-10♠

Position: Cut-off

Blinds: 15/30

Stacks:

UTG	+1	+2	+3	+4	CO	Button	SB	BB
1180	1470	1800	1580	1520	1500	1480	1470	1500
					YOU			

Action

In a tight-aggressive $525 turbo you raise to 90 on the cut-off with J♠-10♠ and are called in the big blind by a tough aggressive player. The flop comes 10♣-9♠-7♠ and after he checks you continuation bet for 150 into the 185 pot. However he now checkraises you to 450. Do you a) fold, b) call or c) move all-in?

Answer

c) move all-in. Not only do you have top pair and a big draw but your opponent is likely capable of check-raising this type of flop as a bluff and may even have a worse hand he will call all-in with. Therefore moving all-in in a simple decision as you will be in good shape whether he calls or folds. Beware, however, of being over-aggressive with weaker combo draws in sitngos, for example if your opponent has 9-8s here he will be in serious trouble if he calls.

21. Playing top pair, no kicker in the big blind in an unraised pot

Game:	$215 9-player turbo sitngo
Players left:	9
Hand:	Q♠-7♣
Position:	Big Blind
Blinds:	10/20
Stacks:	

UTG	+1	+2	+3	+4	CO	Button	SB	BB
1500	1500	1500	1500	1500	1500	1500	1500	1500
								YOU

Action

On the first hand of a $215 turbo there are three limpers to you in the big blind (including the small blind) and you check Q-7o. The flop comes Q♣-8♥-3♦ and you elect to bet 60 into the 80 pot after the small blind checks. However, both limpers call and the small blind folds. The turn is the J♣. Do you a) check and fold to a bet, b) check and call a bet, c) bet and call a raise or d) bet and fold to a raise?

Answer

a) check and fold to a bet. Here you have made a feeler bet to see where you stand (you might also do the same with a hand like A-8), but against two callers the chances that your hand is good are now slim and you are out of position, so this is a good time to give up. If the turn is checked around you should usually check the river too, but be prepared to call a moderate bet most of the time if both cards are blanks.

The middle game

1. Playing a medium pair in early position

Game:	$315 9-player turbo sitngo
Players left:	7
Hand:	8♦-8♣
Position:	UTG
Blinds:	25/50
Stacks:	

UTG	+1	+2	CO	Button	SB	BB
1500	2000	3200	2200	1600	1500	1500
YOU						

Action

There are seven players left in a tight-aggressive $315 turbo and you are dealt 8-8 under-the-gun. Do you a) fold, b) call or c) raise to 150?

Answer

c) raise to 150. As the blinds increase you need to tighten your hand ranges and stop liming speculative hands most of the time, because you are getting worse implied odds and if someone raises behind you, you will usually have to fold. Therefore in early position small pairs and suited connectors should be folded (although you can still limp in late position with pairs after other limpers) but a medium pair like 8-8 should usually be opened with unless you are at a very loose-aggressive table.

2. Playing a strong hand against limpers

Game: $55 9-player turbo sitngo

Players left: 7

Hand: A♦-J♣

Position: Button

Blinds: 25/50

Stacks:

UTG	+1	+2	CO	Button	SB	BB
2000	2000	2200	2000	1900	1800	1600
				YOU		

Action

You are on the button with A-Jo in a $55 turbo. A loose player limps under-the-gun and two other players follow suit. Do you a) fold, b) call, c) raise to 300 or d) raise all-in?

Answer

c) raise to 300. It is unlikely that anyone has a big hand here, so A-Jo is probably winning. You should therefore make a decent-sized raise for value and to force players to pay to draw to their hands and play out of position. There are already 225 chips in the pot, so if everyone folds this adds nicely to your stack, and if there is one caller you should still be able to win the pot frequently with a continuation bet of around 500. Against multiple callers, however, you should not usually bet the flop unless you hit top pair.

3. Playing in late position when everyone has folded

Game: $109 9-player turbo sitngo

Players left: 8

Hand: J♣-8♣

Position: Button

Blinds: 30/60

Stacks:

UTG	+1	+2	+3	CO	Button	SB	BB
1750	1525	1700	1275	2000	1900	1750	1600
					YOU		

Action

Everyone folds to you on the button in a tight-aggressive $109 turbo where you have J-8s. Both you and the big blind are tight-aggressive regulars in these games. Do you a) fold, b) call, c) raise to 180 or d) move all-in?

Answer

c) raise to 180. This is at the lower end of the range with which you should be stealing the blinds, but it is still playable in this situation against a big blind who is unlikely to get involved with many hands, and the blinds are still too low for him to reraise you all-in comfortably. If you are reraised you can easily fold, and if he calls you can still hope to flop a hand or win with a continuation bet. Note, however, that J-8o would be a fold here, and you should probably fold J-8s against a very loose-aggressive big blind.

4 . Playing with deeper stacks

Game: $210 10-player turbo sitngo

Players left: 5

Hand: A♣-A♦

Position: Cut-off

Blinds: 100/200

Stacks:

UTG	CO	Button	SB	BB
1900	3200	3600	3500	2800
	YOU			

Action

Five-handed in a tight-aggressive $210 turbo you have been dealt aces in the cut-off and the first player folds to you. Do you a) fold, b) call, c) raise to 400 d) raise to 500, e) raise to 600 or f) go all-in?

Answer

d) raise to 500. In the middle game you should rarely open to more than three big blinds, and as the blinds rise you may want to lower this to 2.5 big blinds to make raising and continuation betting cheaper and to commit yourself against fewer reraises. This will allow you to fold when players reraise and you have nothing, or let them reraise believing that they have fold equity when you have a monster, as is the case here. You should rarely mini-raise, however, as this makes it too cheap for the big blind to call and if you only do it with a big hand observant players will notice.

5. Playing with awkward stack sizes

Game: $55 9-player turbo sitngo

Players left: 7

Hand: A♠-J♠

Position: Button

Blinds: 40/80

Stacks:

UTG	+1	+2	CO	Button	SB	BB
2080	2000	2240	1920	1920	1800	1540
				YOU		

Action

In a $55 turbo with seven players remaining an unknown player raises to 200 under-the-gun. You have A-Js and the blinds are fairly tight. Do you a) fold, b) call, c) raise to 600 or d) move all-in?

Answer

b) call. A-Js is a strong hand at this stage of a sitngo, but reraising all-in would be a very big raise, and making a smaller reraise would commit you to the calling all-in and make postflop play awkward if you are called. Calling in position to see the flop is therefore the pragmatic option (assuming that the blinds are not likely to make a squeeze reraise) and you can decide from there whether to put any more chips in. Note that you may also smooth call with hands like aces or kings in this situation sometimes if your opponent is unlikely to call a big reraise or if the blinds are aggressive and likely to squeeze.

6. Facing a late position raise

Game: $55 9-player turbo sitngo

Players left: 7

Hand: A♠-J♠

Position: Button

Blinds: 20/40

Stacks:

UTG	+1	+2	CO	Button	SB	BB
2080	2000	2240	1920	1920	1800	1540
				YOU		

Action

The situation is the same as in the hand above except that this time the blinds are 20/40 and the cut-off opens to 120. Do you a) fold, b) call, c) raise to 360 or d) move all-in?

Answer

c) raise to 360. Here the raise has come from a later position player whose hand range will likely be fairly wide and the stacks are deeper in terms of big blinds. Reraising here forces him to fold most of his weaker hands, but you can easily fold if he moves all-in, and if he smooth calls you will still be able to continuation bet the flop for around 400 and fold to a reraise all-in if you have missed.

7. Playing a medium pair out of position

Game: $109 10-player turbo sitngo

Players left: 8

Hand: 7♣-7♦

Position: Small Blind

Blinds: 25/50

Stacks:

UTG	+1	+2	+3	CO	Button	SB	BB
2550	2700	2250	1500	1850	1400	1200	1550
						YOU	

Action

In a tight-aggressive $109 turbo everyone folds to the loose-aggressive cut-off who opens to 150. The button folds and you have 7-7 in the small blind. Do you a) fold, b) call, c) raise to 450 or d) move all-in?

Answer

d) reraise all-in. Although you have a stack of nearly 24 big blinds remaining, you cannot make a smaller raise and continuation bet or call and play out of position comfortably here. Also, since the button is likely to open a wide range of hands and has a similar stack size to you he will not be able to call often, and you will usually pick up the 225 chips in the pot already.

8. Facing a raise with shallow stacks

Game: $15 9-player turbo sitngo

Players left: 7

Hand: A♠-Q♦

Position: Big Blind

Blinds: 50/100

Stacks:

UTG	+1	+2	CO	Button	SB	BB
2050	2000	2050	1950	1900	1800	1750
						YOU

Action

You have A-Qo in the big blind and a mid-position player raises to 300 causing everyone to fold around to you in the big blind. Do you a) fold, b) call or c) move all-in?

Answer

c) move all-in. You have a very strong hand and an ideal sized stack to move all-in with, as you are not risking too many big blinds and are against an opponent will not be able to call with many hands because of his similar stack size. Against looser players A-J and A-10 would also be standard all-ins here, as would most pairs.

9. Facing a reraise from a player with awkward stack sizes

Game: $25 9-player turbo sitngo

Players left: 7

Hand: K♠-Q♠

Position: Button

Blinds: 25/50

Stacks:

UTG	+1	+2	CO	Button	SB	BB
1800	2250	1950	1950	2300	1850	1400
				YOU		

Action

You are playing in a loose-aggressive $25 sitngo and open to 150 on the button with K-Qs. The small blind folds and the big blind, who is a wild and aggressive player, raises to 450. Do you a) fold, b) call, or c) raise all-in?

Answer

b) call. The big blind can have a fairly wide range here and has made a small reraise that only leaves him a pot sized bet on the flop. In this situation therefore he will usually have to commit himself to the pot if he wants to bet postflop and may even move all-in with nothing. If this is the case you will be calling 300 preflop for a chance to win 1575 and when you flop top pair you will rarely be beaten. Note, however, that K-Qs is not a hand to re-reraise all-in with here preflop as you have little fold equity and are unlikely to be dominating his range.

10. Facing a reraise all-in when you are the shorter stack

Game: $100 10-player standard speed sitngo

Players left: 8

Hand: A♦-J♦

Position: UTG+3

Blinds: 50/100

Stacks:

UTG	+1	+2	+3	CO	Button	SB	BB
1050	2000	2250	1500	1900	2950	1800	1550
			YOU				

Action

In a $100 standard speed sitngo everyone folds to you and you open to 250 with A-Jo, but then a very tight player on the button reraises you all-in. It is now 1250 to you to win 1900 and you believe he has a range of 6-6+, A-9s+, A-10o+. Do you a) fold or b) call?

Answer

a) fold. According to ICM if you fold here your $EV will be $88.10 and if you call and win it will be $194.61. Therefore you will need to have over 45.27% equity against your opponent; but against this range you only have 43.91% equity so it is a marginal pass. Note that against a wider reraising range this would be a standard call.

11. Facing a reraise all-in when you are the larger stack

Game: $100 10-player standard speed sitngo

Players left: 8

Hand: A♦-J♦

Position: UTG+3

Blinds: 50/100

Stacks:

UTG	+1	+2	+3	CO	Button	SB	BB
1050	2000	2250	2950	1900	1500	1800	1550
			YOU				

Action

The situation is the same as in the previous hand, except that the stack sizes are now reversed so that you have the deeper stack and have been reraised all-in by a shorter stack on the button. Do you a) fold or b) call?

Answer

b) call. Now you are not facing elimination if you call and lose you have slightly more license to gamble. If you fold your $EV will be $171.54, and calling and winning will increase it to $262.52 whereas calling and losing will reduce it to $100.60. This means that you now only need 43.54% equity or more against the all-in player's range and so can call if his range is still the same.

12. Playing postflop with shallow stacks

Game: $25 9-player standard speed sitngo

Players left: 7

Hand: Q♥-Q♦

Position: UTG

Blinds: 50/100

Stacks:

UTG	+1	+2	CO	Button	SB	BB
2000	2050	2250	1900	1750	1550	2000
YOU						

Action

In a $25 turbo you raise under-the-gun with Q-Q to 250 and are only called by the big blind who is loose-aggressive. The flop comes 4♠-5♥-10♥ and you bet 400 after he checks, which he calls. He against checks to you when the 6♥ comes on the turn and you have 1350 left with the pot standing at 1350. Do you a) check, b) bet 500 or c) go all-in?

Answer

c) go all-in. With shallower stack sizes you can usually get all the money in on the turn if you size your bets correctly, and this will allow you to protect strong one-pair hands from being outdrawn more easily. Although the turn has brought a slightly scary card here, it is unlikely your opponent has check-called the flop with a draw as he could reraise all-in with these stack sizes, and you also have the Q♥ which adds to your equity if you are behind.

13. Facing a raise in the big blind with shallow stacks

Game:	$25 9-player standard speed sitngo
Players left:	7
Hand:	Q♥-J♥
Position:	Big Blind
Blinds:	50/100
Stacks:	

UTG	+1	+2	CO	Button	SB	BB
2000	2050	2250	1900	1750	1550	2000
						YOU

Action

This time you are the big blind and the tight-aggressive cut-off raises to 250, so you elect to call with Q♥-J♥ in the big blind. The flop comes 10♥-7♥-2♣ and after you check the cut-off bets 400 of his remaining 1650 stack. Do you a) fold, b) call or c) move all-in?

Answer

c) move all-in. Although you only have a draw at this stage, the cut-off is likely to continuation bet this flop with any hand he raised with and is by no means committed to calling an all-in. Therefore a good percentage of the time you will win the 950 chips in the pot immediately by moving all-in, and even when called you could still be a favourite if the cut-off has a hand like A-10, and you will only be slightly behind most other strong hands.

14. Playing postflop out of position

Game: $55 9-player standard speed sitngo

Players left: 7

Hand: Q♦-9♠

Position: Small Blind

Blinds: 50/100

Stacks:

UTG	+1	+2	CO	Button	SB	BB
1650	2450	2200	2200	1750	1550	1700
					YOU	

Action

In a $55 turbo everyone folds to you in the small blind and you elect to limp with Q-9o as the big blind is a passive player and you do not want to create a big pot out of position. He checks and the flop comes K♠-5♣-10♦. Do you a) check, b) bet 150 or c) go all-in?

Answer

b) bet 150. You do not need a hand to make this sort of bet on a dry board as it will frequently miss the big blind (your gutshot is a nice bonus). If you are called here, however, you should give up most of the time unless you catch a jack or a queen, and if raised you should just fold.

15. Playing against limpers when the blinds have risen

Game:	$25 9-player turbo sitngo
Players left:	7
Hand:	5♣-5♦
Position:	Button
Blinds:	50/100
Stacks:	

UTG	+1	+2	CO	Button	SB	BB
1650	1950	1700	1700	1750	2550	2200
				YOU		

Action

The first player to act limps despite having a stack of only 16.5 big blinds and is followed by the cut-off, both of whom are loose-passive players. You have 5-5 on the button. Do you a) fold, b) call, c) raise to 400 or d) move all-in?

Answer

b) call. Your read of the limpers it crucial to determining your action here and you must decide what their ranges for limping and for calling an all-in are. Against loose-passive players, who are apt to limp with hands like K-Q or A-9 and then call a large all-in, you would be making a significant mistake by moving all-in here (especially if they also play big pairs in this fashion). However, against players who limp with a wide range but frequently pass to an all-in raise you would move all-in expecting to pick up the dead money most of the time. In this case, however, with the added bonuses of a second limper and position, you would do best to try and flop a set cheaply and get paid off.

16. Playing against a tight-aggressive limper

Game: $210 9-player turbo sitngo

Players left: 7

Hand: A♣-9♠

Position: Button

Blinds: 50/100

Stacks:

UTG	+1	+2	CO	Button	SB	BB
1650	1950	1700	1700	1750	2550	2200
				YOU		

Action

The situation is the same except this time the under-the-gun player folds and a tight-aggressive expert player limps in second position. Everyone folds to you and you have A-9o on the button. Do you a) fold, b) call, c) raise to 400 or d) move all-in.

Answer

a) fold. Here you are up against a player who would not normally be expected to limp at this stage of a sitngo and you should therefore be concerned about his range being mainly very strong hands like A-A which he is hoping to trap someone with if they raise behind him. Because of this you should quickly fold a hand like A-9o since raising would be disastrous if your read is correct, and limping would have terrible reverse implied odds since you will often hit an ace or nine and still lose.

The late game

1. Playing a short stack in late position

Game: $25 9-player turbo sitngo

Players left: 5

Hand: K♠-9♠

Position: Button

Blinds: 100/200

Stacks:

UTG	CO	Button	SB	BB
3300	3650	1800	2550	2200
		YOU		

Action

You are on the button in a $25 turbo with K-9s and two solid players behind you. The action is folded to you, do you a) fold, b) call c) raise to 600 or d) move all-in?

Answer

d) move all-in. The combination of your stack size, hand strength and position make this a standard all-in and most of the time you will increase your stack by a sixth when they fold, which would be very useful since you are last in chips.

2. Playing a short stack in mid-position

Game: $50 9-player turbo sitngo

Players left: 7

Hand: A♣-J♠

Position: UTG+1

Blinds: 100/200

Stacks:

UTG	+1	+2	CO	Button	SB	BB
1600	2000	1700	2000	1750	2550	1900
	YOU					

Action

You have five players behind you in a $50 turbo and have been dealt A-Jo. Do you a) fold, b) call, c) raise to 500 or d) move all-in?

Answer

d) move all-in. Although you are risking 2000 to win 300 with a lot of players left to act, your hand is definitely strong enough to do so. Note, however, that A-10o would be marginal here and that A-9o would be a fold against most sensible calling ranges.

3. Playing a small pair in early position

Game: $5 10-player turbo sitngo

Players left: 8

Hand: 2♥-2♦

Position: UTG

Blinds: 100/200

Stacks:

UTG	+1	+2	+3	CO	Button	SB	BB
2000	1600	1700	2000	2000	1750	2050	1900
YOU							

Action

You are under-the-gun in a $5 turbo with eight players left and 2-2. Do you a) fold, b) call c) raise to 500 or d) move all-in?

Answer

a) Fold. Against this many players moving all-in would only be profitable if they called with the top 4% of all hands (A-Q+, 10-10+) which you cannot expect to be accurate, especially in a game with this buy-in. It is simply not worth risking your chips in this spot against this number of players when you will either be in a coin-flip or way behind when called.

4. Playing a deep stack in early position

Game: $15 10-player turbo sitngo

Players left: 8

Hand: 10♠-10♦

Position: UTG

Blinds: 75/150

Stacks:

UTG	+1	+2	+3	CO	Button	SB	BB
2000	1600	1700	2000	2000	1750	2050	1900
YOU							

Action

You are under-the-gun in a $15 turbo with 10-10 and almost 14 big blinds against a table of players with 10 big blinds or more. Do you a) fold, b) call, c) raise to 375 or d) move all-in?

Answer

d) Move all-in. Although you are now risking 2000 to win only 225 your hand is so strong that you stand to profit here in almost all scenarios, and raising all-in also removes the possibility of getting in an awkward situation postflop.

5. Facing a raise all-in with a medium pair

Game: $105 9-player turbo sitngo

Players left: 6

Hand: 8♣-8♦

Position: Big Blind

Blinds: 100/200

Stacks:

UTG	+1	CO	Button	SB	BB
1600	2000	2000	1750	2550	3600
					YOU

Action

You are in the big blind in a $105 turbo when the button pushes all-in for almost nine big blinds. You cover his stack by some way and have 8-8. Do you a) fold or b) call?

Answer

b) Call. This is a straightforward call against most button all-in ranges, as you will sometimes dominate smaller pairs or weak aces, have good pot odds, and have additional chips so that you are not eliminated if you lose. You should, however, be wary of calling here with small pairs and weak aces that will rarely dominate another hand and may be dominated them-selves.

6. Facing two all-ins with a medium pair

Game: $210 9-player turbo sitngo

Players left: 7

Hand: 10♥-10♠

Position: Big Blind

Blinds: 100/200

Stacks:

UTG	+1	+2	CO	Button	SB	BB
1600	2000	1700	2000	1750	2550	1900
						YOU

Action

In a $210 turbo with 10-10 in the big blind the first player to act goes all-in and the cut-off raises all-in over the top of him. It is 1700 to you in the big blind to win 3800. Do you a) fold or b) call?

Answer

a) fold. Although you are getting attractive odds to call here, your hand is rarely in good shape against two players with these stack sizes. The under-the-gun raiser will usually have a very tight range, and the cut-off will know this and so his range will be even tighter, meaning that you will often see an overpair and almost always overcards like A-K or A-Q. Also, even though you would end up with a big stack here if you won it would not be worth anywhere near three times the $EV of your current stack for ICM reasons, and so the pot odds you are getting are much less attractive than they might seem.

7. Facing a small raise with a strong hand in the big blind

Game:	$200 10-player turbo sitngo
Players left:	8
Hand:	A♥-J♠
Position:	Big Blind
Blinds:	100/200
Stacks:	

UTG	+1	+2	+3	CO	Button	SB	BB
2000	1600	1700	2000	2000	1750	2050	1900
							YOU

Action

You have A-Jo on the big blind a $200 turbo when a very solid player opens to 500 under-the-gun. Do you a) fold, b) call or c) raise all-in?

Answer

a) fold. This size of raise from a solid opponent who will usually play an all-in or fold strategy in the late game, and has stack of ten big blinds in early position, is very suspicious. Unless you have seen him do this regularly, you are probably crushed here and should fold even though your hand is very strong and you have excellent pot odds to call.

8. Playing with antes

Game: $60 10-player turbo sitngo

Players left: 8

Hand: 6♥-6♦

Position: UTG

Blinds: 100/200/a25

Stacks:

UTG	+1	+2	+3	CO	Button	SB	BB
2000	1600	1700	2000	2000	1750	2050	1900
YOU							

Action

You have 6-6 under-the-gun in a $60 turbo with eight players remaining. Do you a) fold, b) call, c) raise to 500 or d) move all-in?

Answer

d) move all-in. Although you would normally fold small pairs in early position for 10 big blinds, with antes in play there are now 500 chips in each pot, making the blinds more like 150/300 and your stack equivalent to less than seven big blinds. This additional incentive makes pushing here standard.

9. Getting good pot odds in the big blind

Game:	$60 10-player turbo sitngo
Players left:	8
Hand:	Q♠-7♠
Position:	Big Blind
Blinds:	100/200/a25
Stacks:	

UTG	+1	+2	+3	CO	Button	SB	BB
2000	1600	1700	3000	2000	750	2050	1900
							YOU

Action

In another $60 turbo you are in the big blind with Q-7s and the button pushes all-in, making it 525 to you to win 1225. Do you a) fold or b) call?

Answer

b) call. Although you don't have a great hand, you are getting almost 2.5-1 pot odds and will still have a playable stack if you lose, whereas winning will give you the chip lead. This would be a good opportunity to gamble and try to pick up some of the dead money in the pot.

10. Playing against the big blind from the small blind

Game:	$300 9-player turbo sitngo
Players left:	6
Hand:	10♠-9♦
Position:	Small Blind
Blinds:	120/240
Stacks:	

UTG	+1	CO	Button	SB	BB
2600	2000	2000	2380	1920	2600
				YOU	

Action

You are in the small blind in a $300 turbo with eight big blinds when everyone folds to you and you are up against a solid player in the big blind. Do you a) fold, b) call, c raise to 720 or d) move all-in?

Answer

d) move all-in. Although your hand is not fantastic, it plays well against a standard all-in calling range and the big blind will not be able to call with many hands for ICM reasons, meaning that most of the time you will pick up the 360 chips in the middle. If the big blind only calls with the top 34% of all hands (2-2+, A-2+, K-5o+, K-2s+, Q-10o+, Q-8s+, J-9s+) this will be a profitable all-in.

11. Facing an all-in from the small blind

Game: $300 9-player turbo sitngo

Players left: 5

Hand: A♠-2♦

Position: Big Blind

Blinds: 120/240

Stacks:

UTG	CO	Button	SB	BB
2600	4000	2380	1920	2600
				YOU

Action

In a similar game you are now the big blind and everyone folds to the small blind, who is a tight-passive player but moves all-in. You must call 1680 to win 2160. Do you a) fold or b) call?

Answer

a) fold. Although against an aggressive player you would call here, against a tight or passive one you should fold, as you are not getting very attractive odds and ICM concerns will far outweigh them. Your opponent would need to be shoving the top 56% or more of all hands for calling to be profitable.

12. Playing against limpers with short stacks

Game: $10 10-player turbo sitngo

Players left: 8

Hand: 8♣-8♦

Position: Button

Blinds: 100/200/a25

Stacks:

UTG	+1	+2	+3	CO	Button	SB	BB
1600	2000	1850	1500	1700	1600	2550	2200
					YOU		

Action

You are on the button with 8-8 in a $10 turbo sitngo when the first player to act limps and is followed by the cut-off, both of whom are loose-passive and often play this way. Do you a) fold, b) call or c) move all-in?

Answer

c) move all-in. Here there are already 900 in the pot to win if both players fold, and with these dead chips as overlay and so many players still in the game it would not be a disaster if you were called by a player with overcards. Your opponents are not likely to have bigger pairs here, and if you fold you will still need to move all-in soon anyway, with the blinds and antes costing 500 per round.

The bubble

1. Under-the-gun with a short stack

Game:	$55 9-player standard speed sitngo
Players left:	4
Hand:	J♠-10♣
Position:	UTG
Blinds:	150/300
Stacks:	

UTG	Button	SB	BB
1800	2650	3550	5500
YOU			

Action

In a $55 turbo you are the short stack with six big blinds and are under-the-gun with J-10o. Do you a) fold, b) call, c) raise to 900 or d) go all-in?

Answer

d) go all-in. Moving all-in or folding is your best option at this stage and, since you are last in chips on the bubble, pushing with any playable hand is standard here as you need to stay in contention with the other players. If your opponents call with only the top 10% of all hands (5-5+, A-10o+, A-8s+, K-Qs) this will be a profitable all-in according to ICM.

2. Under-the-gun with a very short stack

Game: $25 10-player turbo sitngo

Players left: 4

Hand: K♥-7♣

Position: UTG

Blinds: 200/400

Stacks:

UTG	Button	SB	BB
1900	4500	4000	4600
YOU			

Action

You are under-the-gun in a $25 turbo with 1900 chips at the 200/400 level and are dealt K-7o. Do you a) fold or b) go all-in?

Answer

b) go all-in. Not only are you the shortest stack, but with less than five big blinds if you go through the blinds again, you will lose a significant portion of your stack and have no fold equity when you do push all-in. Although you have a marginal hand, it is well above average and the big blind will have to call 1500 to win 2500 if the other players fold, so he will usually fold a good proportion of the time, allowing you to win the pot without a showdown.

3. Playing from the small blind with similar stack sizes

Game:	$210 10-player turbo sitngo
Players left:	4
Hand:	3-20
Position:	Small Blind
Blinds:	200/400
Stacks:	

UTG	Button	SB	BB
3825	3975	3600	3600
		YOU	

Action

In a tight-aggressive $210 turbo with blinds of 200/400 you find the action folded to you in the small blind with 3-2 offsuit against a solid player in the big blind. Do you a) fold, b) call, c) raise to 1000 or d) go all-in?

Answer

d) go all-in. You should go all-in here irrespective of your two cards, assuming that the big blind is a competent sitngo player who understands ICM and bubble strategy. This is profitable because the blinds are so high, and the range of hands the big blind can call with is so low, that most of the time you will win an extra 600 chips, and still have a chance to win even when called. It also means that when you win the blinds you now can't be knocked out, which puts you in a much stronger position for the next hand, where you can push against two players with more hands based on that knowledge and try to build a dominating lead.

4. Facing an all-in from the small blind with equal stacks

Game: $55 10-player turbo sitngo

Players left: 4

Hand: A♥-8♣

Position: Big Blind

Blinds: 200/400/a25

Stacks:

UTG	Button	SB	BB
3700	3500	4200	3600
			YOU

Action

In a $55 turbo everyone folds to the aggressive small blind who immediately goes all-in. You have A-8o in the big blind. Do you a) fold or b) call?

Answer

a) fold. Although you suspect the small blind would push 100% of hands here and that A-8o is well ahead of that range (it would have 59.87% equity against a random hand), there is nothing you can do here but fold for ICM reasons, since the equity you gain by calling and winning is far less that that which you lose when you are eliminated and the other players get a free pass to the money stages.

5. Playing a medium strength hand on the button

Game: $25 10-player turbo sitngo

Players left: 4

Hand: 10♠-9♥

Position: Button

Blinds: 300/600/a50

Stacks:

UTG	Button	SB	BB
3600	3900	3600	3900
	YOU		

Action

You are tied for the chip lead in a $25 turbo against three tight players and have 10-9o on the button. Do you a) fold or b) move all-in?

Answer

b) move all-in. Although you do not have a premium hand, unsuited connectors play well in all-in situations, and if you win this hand you will open up a chip lead that you can exploit further in the next hand with the intention of building a dominating stack and going on to win the event.

6. Playing the big stack against three smaller stacks

Game: $55 9-player turbo sitngo

Players left: 4

Hand: 7♦-4♣

Position: Button

Blinds: 200/400/a25

Stacks:

UTG	Button	SB	BB
2560	6440	1650	2850
	YOU		

Action

You are the big stack after winning an all-in and are dealt 7-4o on the button in a $55 turbo. The first player folds and you are left up against two reasonable sitngo players in the blinds who understand bubble play intuitively and are unlikely to make any huge mistakes. Do you a) fold, b) raise to 1000 or c) go all-in?

Answer

c) go all-in. Although 7-4o is a terrible hand in a vacuum, you are in a fantastic situation and with a massive chip lead on the bubble you should aim to accumulate as many chips as possible before the bubble bursts. The small blind only has 200 invested and having just paid the blinds can afford to wait for a better opportunity unless he picks up a big hand, and the big blind, who is in second place overall, has a lot to lose by being eliminated and so will fold all but the strongest hands.

7. Playing the big stack when there is a micro-stack

Game:	$555 9-player turbo sitngo
Players left:	4
Hand:	3♠-2♣
Position:	Button
Blinds:	100/200
Stacks:	

UTG	Button	SB	BB
200	5500	4200	3600
	YOU		

Action

You have just taken the chip lead and crippled another player in a $555 turbo and now have 3-2o on the button against two deeper stacks and one micro-stack. The micro-stack folds. Do you a) fold, b) call) c) raise to 1200 or d) move all-in?

Answer

d) move all-in. Although the other players still have over 15 big blinds, with the micro-stack about to face the big blind, they will be unable to call an all-in with anything apart from the biggest pairs, and you should therefore use this opportunity to pick up the blinds without risking a confrontation.

8. Playing against a big stack

Game: $15 10-player turbo sitngo

Players left: 4

Hand: A♥-Q♣

Position: Small Blind

Blinds: 200/400/a25

Stacks:

UTG	Button	SB	BB
7700	2200	2500	2600
		YOU	

Action

In a $15 turbo there is one big stack and three smaller stacks left on the bubble. The big stack has been playing a passive game during the early stages but has just doubled up. He opens to 1200 and you have A-Qo in the small blind. Do you a) fold, b) call or c) raise all-in?

Answer

a) fold. Although you have some chips committed and are likely ahead of his opening range, you are in competition with the other short stacks and not this player, whose raise effectively commits you to playing all-in or folding. Big cards do poorly in situations like this on the bubble, as most hands will be live against them and you are not getting the same pot odds as you would in the big blind, where the decision would be much closer.

9. Facing an all-in from the big stack in second place

Game: $109 10-player standard speed sitngo

Players left: 4

Hand: A♠-K♠

Position: Big Blind

Blinds: 150/300

Stacks:

UTG	Button	SB	BB
1500	1500	9000	3000
			YOU

Action

In a $109 turbo with blinds of 150-300 you are in second place overall and in the big blind. The short stacks fold and the aggressive big stack pushes all-in from the small blind. You have A-Ks. Do you a) fold or b) call all-in?

Answer

a) fold. Even if your opponent is moving all-in every time here you should still be folding all hands in this spot except high pairs like A-A, K-K or Q-Q, which are able to dominate two undercards. A-K on the other hand will not fare so well against two random cards with only 67.05% equity since they will often be live, and being eliminated almost one-third of the time here would be a disaster given the existence of the two short stacks.

10. Playing a micro-stack after a raise

Game: $50 9-player turbo sitngo

Players left: 9

Hand: 2♦-2♠

Position: Button

Blinds: 300/600

Stacks:

UTG	Button	SB	BB
7500	900	2700	3900
	YOU		

Action

In a $50 turbo you have just been crippled and left with 900 chips. The big stack created by that hand pushes all-in under-the-gun on the next hand and you have 2-2 on the button. Do you a) fold or b) call?

Answer

b) call. Although in most situations calling with small pairs is not advisable, here the raiser's range will usually be very wide and you are getting excellent pot odds to triple through and get yourself immediately back into the action, since the blinds will usually fold, leaving you against only the big stack.

11. Under-the-gun with a micro-stack

Game: $50 10-player turbo sitngo

Players left: 4

Hand: Q♥-8♣

Position: UTG

Blinds: 300/600

Stacks:

UTG	Button	SB	BB
900	7500	2700	3900
YOU			

Action

The situation is the same as above however this time you are under-the-gun with 1.5 big blinds and Q-8o. Do you a) fold or b) go all-in?

Answer

a) fold. Although Q-8o is a better than average hand and you will be getting good pot odds from the dead money in the pot if only the big blind calls, you should still fold here unless you have at least a fairly strong hand as you will have to take the big blind on the next hand if you win anyway, and that will eat up a big proportion of the chips you have just won.

12. Facing an all-in from another big stack

Game: $111 9-player turbo sitngo

Players left: 4

Hand: Q-Q

Position: Big Blind

Blinds: 200/400/a25

Stacks:

UTG	Button	SB	BB
5000	2000	1500	5000
			YOU

Action

Both you and another player are deep stacked with two short stacks having the remaining chips. The other big stack is an expert sitngo player and moves all-in under-the-gun. You have Q-Q in the big blind. Do you a) fold or b) call?

Answer

b) call. Although some players might advocate folding, an expert will know that he can profitably move all-in under-the-gun here with almost any two cards since the blinds are high, the short stacks can do him little damage, and you can only call and risk elimination with a small number of hands. Because of this, even though there is a player with only three big blinds remaining you should still be happy to call here and risk elimination since Q-Q will dominate his hand totally unless he has an ace or king, making it massively profitable according to ICM. Note that in situations where ICM suggests calling might only be slightly profitable that you should usually fold because of the presence of the short stack.

13. Playing against your closest rival's big blind

Game: $12 10-player turbo sitngo

Players left: 4

Hand: Q♥-6♥

Position: Button

Blinds: 300/600/a50

Stacks:

UTG	Button	SB	BB
5700	2700	3600	3000
	YOU		

Action

In a $12 turbo with blinds of 300/600/a50 you are down to less than five big blinds and on the button with Q-6s. The under-the-gun player has folded, leaving you up against the small and big blinds. Do you a) fold b) call or c) go all-in?

Answer

c) go all-in. Q-6s might not be the strongest of hands, but it is above average and every situational aspect of your position dictates that this is the time to move all-in with it. The small blind can comfortably fold unless he has a monster, and whilst your closest rival in the big blind will be getting good pot odds he will be crippled if he calls and loses. Also, if you give up this hand you won't have enough chips to go through the blinds again without losing a lot of your stack and fold equity, and so you will have to move all-in with many hands under-the-gun anyway. However, this situation will be much worse as it is the big stack's big blind, who will be able to call you with more ease and whom you gain less by winning chips from.

14. Facing an all-in from your closest rival

Game: $210 9-player turbo sitngo

Players left: 4

Hand: 5♣-5♠

Position: Big Blind

Blinds: 200/400/a25

Stacks:

UTG	Button	SB	BB
4200	2750	4100	2450
			YOU

Action

In a $210 turbo you are in the big blind with 5-5 when the under-the-gun player folds and the tough-aggressive button who is your closest rival moves all-in, causing the small blind to fold. You have 2025 left after posting. Do you a) fold or b) call?

Answer

b) call. This appears to be a tough spot as you will rarely be dominating your opponent's hand. However, you are getting good odds to call and have the opportunity to cripple your closest rival if you win the hand, whereas if you fold you will have nearly half as many chips as him after posting the small blind on the next hand and will be the favourite to bubble anyway.

15. Playing a medium stack against a micro-stack

Game: $25 10-player turbo sitngo

Players left: 4

Hand: A♥-2♠

Position: Small Blind

Blinds: 300/600

Stacks:

UTG	Button	SB	BB
9400	2400	2600	600
		YOU	

Action

In a $25 turbo you are in the small blind with a little over four big blinds when the button limps after the big stack has folded under the gun. There is a micro-stack all-in in the big blind. Do you a) fold, b) call, c) raise to 1,800 or d) move all-in?

Answer

b) call. Although moving all-in would often force the limper to fold and allow you to play heads-up against the big blind, you should prefer to keep him in and co-operate in trying to end the bubble as quickly as possible since you gain more $EV from this strategy when your hand is not all that strong against a random hand.

16. Under-the-gun facing a blind increase on the next hand

Game: $50 9-player turbo sitngo

Players left: 4

Hand: 10♠-8♠

Position: UTG

Blinds: 100/200/a25

Stacks:

UTG	Button	SB	BB
1800	5300	2500	3900
YOU			

Action

You are under-the-gun in a $50 turbo with nine big blinds and the shortest stack, but the blinds are about to rise to 200/400/a25 on the next hand. Do you a) fold, b) call, c) raise to 600 or d) move all-in?

Answer

d) move all-in. This play would be +$EV according to ICM if your opponents only call with the top 10% of all hands (5-5+, A-10o+, A-8s+, K-Qs+), but even if the true figure was slightly higher than this it would still be correct to move all-in, as ICM does not account for the impact of the blinds on your overall chances in the game. Here, if you fold you will have to put over 20% of your stack in on the next hand and be decimated, but if you move all-in and win the blinds you will then have a stack of 2175 and be able to scrape through the blinds and maintain some fold equity for the next round.

17. Playing with antes

Game: $315 9-player turbo sitngo

Players left: 4

Hand: A♣-5♣

Position: UTG

Blinds: 100/200/a25

Stacks:

UTG	Button	SB	BB
2000	5500	2500	3500
YOU			

Action

Under-the-gun in a $315 turbo you are dealt A-5s with antes in play. Do you a) fold, b) call c) raise to 600 or d) move all-in?

Answer

d) move all-in. This play would be fractionally +$EV if your opponents only call with the top 9% of all hands (6-6+, A-10o+, A-9s+), but with no antes and only 300 chips in the pot as opposed to 400 it would be significantly -$EV against the same calling ranges, as the amount you are risking your entire stack to win is reduced by 25%.

18. Facing a small raise when you have a big stack

Game: $111 9-player standard speed sitngo

Players left: 4

Hand: 7♥-6♥

Position: Button

Blinds: 100/200/a25

Stacks:

UTG	Button	SB	BB
3100	5900	1750	2750
	YOU		

Action

You have 7-6s on the button and have recently acquired a big stack against unfamiliar opposition who all seem to be competent sitngo players. A loose-aggressive under-the-gun player, who has been raising a lot, opens to 500. Do you a) fold, b) call or c) go all-in?

Answer

c) go all-in. Although your hand is not a premium one, with the stack sizes as they are you have massive fold equity against any player who has made a standard sized raise and there are 900 chips on offer for you to pick up. When your opponent folds to an all-in, your equity will increase by about $24, and when called by the raiser it will increase by about $86 if you win the all-in and decrease by about $104 if you lose. Against a calling range like J-J+, A-Q+, you will have almost 33% equity so you will lose an average of $40.67 when called by this player, but if everyone folds more than about 63% of the time you will show a profit.

19. Playing against inexperienced opposition

Game: $1 10-player turbo sitngo

Players left: 4

Hand: 5♠-4♦

Position: Small Blind

Blinds: 200/400/a25

Stacks:

UTG	Button	SB	BB
4000	4000	3500	3500
		YOU	

Action

You are on the small blind of a $1 turbo sitngo and everyone folds to you with 5-4o, leaving you against the big blind who is a very loose and inexperienced sitngo player. Do you a) fold, b) call c) raise to 1200 or d) go all-in?

Answer

a) fold. Although against good players you can move all-in with 100% of hands here and with 5-4o it will be profitable if the big blind only calls with the top 19% of all hands (3-3+, A-5o+, A-2s+, K-Qo, K-10s+) if he is very loose his range may be wider than this making your all-in unprofitable. Note that the big blind's call here with a wider range than advisable would cost him money too, but that since there is nothing you can do about it you must simply adapt your strategy and not push with hands at the bottom of your range.

20. Playing the chip lead when the blinds are deep

Game: $100 10-player standard speed sitngo

Players left: 4

Hand: Q♠-J♦

Position: Button

Blinds: 100/200/a25

Stacks:

UTG	Button	SB	BB
4000	4000	3500	3500
	YOU		

Action

In a standard speed sitngo where everyone still has 15 or more big blinds, the first player folds and you have Q-Jo on the button. Do you a) fold, b) call, c) raise to 500 or d) move all-in?

Answer

c) raise to 500. Although moving all-in here will usually be +$EV, making a small raise should be even more profitable since you will be only risking 500 to win 400 and can fold to a reraise or make a flop continuation bet without committing to the hand if called and checked to. If your opponents are fairly tight-passive, you should easily be able to use this strategy to build a chip lead with little risk and have a dominating stack by the time the blinds rise or the other players stacks diminish to a point where you can use an aggressive all-in strategy.

21. Playing postflop when the stacks are deep

Game: $100 10-player standard speed sitngo

Players left: 4

Hand: Q♠-J♦

Position: Button

Blinds: 100/200/a25

Stacks:

UTG	Button	SB	BB
4000	4000	3500	3500
	YOU		

Action

In the same situation as above you raise to 500 on the button and are called in the big blind buy a tight solid player. The flop comes K-Q-4 rainbow and he checks to you. Do you a) check, b) bet 800 or d) move all-in?

Answer

a) check. Although you have more chips than your opponent here, losing a big pot will still cripple you. For this reason you should proceed cautiously postflop and not look to put all your chips in without a very strong hand. Here you have made second pair, which is likely ahead, but if you bet and are called or raised you will be in a tough spot. By checking you will control the size of the pot in a situation where there are few cards that are likely to put your opponent in front if he is not in front already, and you may even induce a bluff from him on a later street. Your general plan should be to call a bet on the turn or bet if checked to (unless an ace comes), but not make or call a second sizable bet on the river against most opponents unless you improve your hand or he is very likely to be bluffing.

In the money (playing three-handed)

1. Adjusting to three-handed play

Game: $10 9-player turbo speed sitngo

Players left: 3

Hand: 3♠-2♦

Position: Small Blind

Blinds: 200/400/a25

Stacks:

Button	SB	BB
4500	4500	4500
	YOU	

Action

In a $10 turbo, where all players have equal stacks of slightly more than 11 big blinds, the button folds and you are in the small blind with 3-2o. Do you a) fold, b) call, c) raise to 1200 or d) move all-in?

Answer

a) fold. Now that the bubble has burst you have far less leverage against your opponents as they will be playing to win rather than to move up to second. If you push with 3-2o here then it will be profitable against players who only call with the top 19% of all hands (3-3+, A-5o+, A-2s+, K-Qo, K-10s+), but many players would call with any ace or pair here and widen their ranges even further if they suspect that you are playing over-aggressively.

2. Playing a short stack

Game: $50 9-player turbo sitngo

Players left: 3

Hand: 10♠-7♦

Position: Button

Blinds: 200/400/a25

Stacks:

Button	SB	BB
1800	8200	3500
YOU		

Action

You have successfully survived the bubble of a $50 turbo but have been left very short stacked under-the-gun. You are dealt 10-7o. Do you a) fold, b) call or c) raise all-in?

Answer

c) raise all-in. At this point you have accomplished your main goal of cashing for 20% of the prize pool, and you have little left to lose by gambling with the remainder of your chips in an attempt to get back in the game. Here you have an ideal situation to push with a wide range as you can attack the second-place player in the big blind and still have some fold equity, as he will have to call 1375 to win 2450, plus if you fold you will be in the big blind on the next hand anyway.

3. Playing a big stack

Game: $50 9-player turbo speed sitngo

Players left: 3

Hand: 3♥-2♦

Position: Small Blind

Blinds: 200/400/a25

Stacks:

Button	SB	BB
1800	8200	3500
	YOU	

Action

In the same game as above you are the big stack on the small blind and the short-stacked button has folded. Do you a) fold, b) call, c) raise to 1200 or d) move all-in?

Answer

d) move all-in. Here, although the bubble has burst, with the presence of a short stack the big blind still has an incentive to play conservatively in order to move up to second and will need a very strong hand to risk being eliminated in third by you.

4. Facing an all-in when there is a micro-stack

Game:	$210 9-player turbo speed sitngo
Players left:	3
Hand:	A♠-J♥
Position:	Big Blind
Blinds:	200/400/a25
Stacks:	

Button	SB	BB
800	8200	4500
		YOU

Action

You are in second place in a $210 turbo with a micro-stack on the button who has folded. The big stack has pushed all-in from the small blind and you have A-Jo. Do you a) fold or b) call?

Answer

a) fold. As we saw, on the bubble you should not play many hands when there is the prospect of a player busting out in the immediate future and increasing your equity with no risk. Here A-Jo is about neutral $EV according to ICM if the small blind moves all-in with 100% of his range, but with the prospect of the button being eliminated on the next hand and guaranteeing you second-place money, folding becomes an easy decision. Notice that with the emphasis on playing to win at this stage of the tournament you would not fold a hand like A-K or 8-8 here, which you might have done on the bubble.

5. Facing a raise when the blinds are deep

Game: $60 9-player standard speed sitngo

Players left: 3

Hand: J♠-10♠

Position: Big Blind

Blinds: 120/240

Stacks:

Button	SB	BB
5100	4200	4200
		YOU

Action

In a $60 standard speed sitngo where the blinds are 120/240 you are in the big blind with Q-Js. The button folds and the tight-aggressive small blind raises to 720. Do you a) fold, b) call or c) move all-in?

Answer

c) move all-in. At this stage you should be playing to win and trying to accumulate chips wherever possible. Here you have a hand that plays well all-in, and fold equity against a player who may just be trying to steal the blinds cheaply and must call 3480 to win 4920. There is 960 in the middle to win uncontested, and even when called you will still have reasonable equity most of the time.

6. Playing a draw postflop when the stacks are deep

Game: $60 9-player standard speed sitngo

Players left: 9

Hand: J♠-10♠

Position: Big Blind

Blinds: 120/240

Stacks:

Button	SB	BB
5100	4200	4200
		YOU

Action

In the same hand you elect to just call your opponent's raise and see a flop of 9♣-Q♠-2♦. The pot is 1440 with you both having 3480 behind, and your opponent continuation bets for 720. Do you a) fold, b) call or c) raise all-in?

Answer

c) raise all-in. Whilst making a move like this on the bubble would be very risky, in this situation it will usually be profitable since your opponent's range for raising preflop and continuation betting will be very wide and you should be playing to win now that you are in the money. You are risking your remaining 3480 to win 2160 in a situation where most of the time your opponent will not be able to continue, and even when he does call you will usually have around eight outs to win.

Heads-up (one-on-one)

1. Playing in a cash game freezeout

Game:	$225 9-player turbo
Players left:	2
Hand:	Q♣-8♠
Position:	Big Blind
Blinds:	100/200
Stacks:	

SB	BB
9100	4400
	YOU

Action

You are facing a maniac who moves all-in every hand from the small blind and have Q-8o and 22 big blinds. Do you a) fold or b) call?

Answer

b) call. Since you are only competing for the remaining prize money your $EV and your cEV are now identical, so you simply need to consider the pot odds you are getting and your equity in the hand. Q-8o is almost 54% against a random hand and you are calling 4200 to win 4600, so you have an easy call here.

2. Playing against a tough opponent

Game: $525 9-player turbo sitngo

Players left: 2

Hand: J♥-3♥

Position: Small Blind

Blinds: 300/600

Stacks:

SB	BB
6100	7400
YOU	

Action

You are dealt J-3s in the small blind with 6100 chips, against a tough sitngo pro in the big blind. Do you a) fold, b) call, c) raise to 1800 or d) move all-in?

Answer

d) move all-in. As you will see from the jam or fold tables on pages 101-2, J-3s has a maximum pushing value of 10.6 big blinds and you have less than this so you should move all-in. This will surprise many players, but the suited nature of your hand is enough to make it worth playing here (J-3o is only worth pushing with five big blinds or less), and roughly equivalent in value to a hand like 9-7o or Q-7o.

2. Facing an all-in from a tough opponent

Game: $525 9-player turbo sitngo

Players left: 2

Hand: K♣-5♦

Position: Big Blind

Blinds: 300/600

Stacks:

SB	BB
7400	6100
	YOU

Action

Against the same opponent you are dealt K♣-5♦ in the big blind with 6100 chips and blinds of 300/600. He moves all-in, covering you. Do you a) fold or b) call?

Answer

b) call. Again this may surprise many players, but with these stack sizes an optimally playing opponent will be pushing with a massive range of hands, many of which are worse than king-high, plus you are calling 5500 to win 6700. For this reason K-5o has a maximum calling value of 10.3 big blinds, and has similar worth in calling to a hand like Q-7s or J-8s.

3. Facing an all-in from a tight opponent

Game: $27 9-player turbo sitngo

Players left: 2

Hand: 2♠-2♥

Position: Big Blind

Blinds: 200/400

Stacks:

SB	BB
7500	6000
	YOU

Action

You are playing against a very tight player heads-up and have 15 big blinds. He pushes all-in and covers you. Do you a) fold or b) call?

Answer

b) fold. Against an optimally-playing opponent, calling here with 2-2 would be barely profitable with a maximum calling value of 15.1 big blinds. However, against a player who is clearly tighter than that you should certainly fold marginal hands like this as his range will be more weighted towards pairs that have you crushed and the pot odds you are getting will not compensate for this.

4. Playing against a tight opponent from the button

Game: $27 9-player turbo sitngo

Players left: 2

Hand: 3♥-2♠

Position: Small Blind

Blinds: 300/600

Stacks:

SB	BB
6000	7500
YOU	

Action

Against the same tight player with blinds having increased to 300/600, you are dealt 3-2o in the small blind with 10 big blinds and believe that he will wait for an ace or pair to call you with. Do you a) fold, b) call, c) raise to 1800 or d) move all-in?

Answer

d) move all-in. If the blinds were still 200/400 then raising to 1200 would be reasonable if it would force your opponent to fold a similar range to an all-in, but with 10 big blinds you should usually revert to a push or fold strategy. Here you can push with 100% of hands if your opponent calls with only the top 26% of all hands (2-2+, A-2+, K-9o+, K-7s+, Q-10s+, J-10s).

5. Adjusting for antes

Game:	$225 9-player turbo sitngo
Players left:	2
Hand:	J♣-2♣
Position:	Small Blind
Blinds:	300/600/a75
Stacks:	

SB	BB
6000	7500
YOU	

Action

You are heads-up against an opponent who you have little information on but hasn't made any mistakes so far with a stack of 10 big blinds. You are dealt J-2s. Do you a) fold, b) call, c) raise to 1800 or d) move all-in?

Answer

d) move all-in. Although J-2s has a maximum pushing value of 8.8 big blinds, in this situation with antes in play it is still playable since there is 1050 in the pot, which is roughly equivalent to 350/700 blinds, meaning that you should consider your stack to be roughly equivalent to 8.6 rather than 10 big blinds.

6. Playing heads-up with low blinds

Game: $114 9-player turbo sitngo

Players left: 2

Hand: A♠-2♣

Position: Small Blind

Blinds: 100/200

Stacks:

SB	BB
5200	8300
YOU	

Action

You are playing a tight-passive opponent with deep stacks and are dealt A-2o in the small blind. Do you a) fold, b) call, c) raise to 600 or d) raise all-in?

Answer

c) raise to 600. Although A-2o has a maximum pushing value of 29.2 big blinds and you are well within that range, against this player you are likely to accomplish a similar amount with a raise to 600 rather than one to 5200, since he is still likely to fold the majority of the time, but when he does find a strong hand you will lose considerably less chips. Also, you don't even really mind if this player calls your raise to 600 with a few more hands, as the majority of the time he will miss the flop and fold to your continuation bet.

7. Considering your pot odds

Game:	$225 9-player turbo sitngo
Players left:	2
Hand:	A♣-7♠
Position:	Small Blind
Blinds:	100/200
Stacks:	

SB	BB
9000	4500
YOU	

Action

You have just reached the heads-up stage and are playing against a very loose-aggressive opponent whom you have no experience with at this stage of a sitngo. On the first hand you raise from the button to 600 with A-7o and he goes all-in for 4500, making it 3900 to you to win 5100. Do you a) fold or b) call?

Answer

b) call. Since you are playing heads-up, there are no ICM considerations to worry about here and you simply need to consider whether you are getting the correct pot odds to call. Calling 3900 to win 5100 you will need to have over 43.33% equity against his range to show a profit, but against any pair or any ace you will only have 40.81%. However, if he will also move all-in with any face cards (K-Q, K-J and Q-J) then our equity rises to 43.63%, and even further if smaller suited connectors or other hands are added. Since an aggressive opponent is likely to reraise with these extra hands, calling should be a profitable decision.

8. Playing a small pair with deep stacks

Game: $225 9-player turbo sitngo

Players left: 2

Hand: 2♣-2♠

Position: Small Blind

Blinds: 100/200

Stacks:

SB	BB
10,000	3500
YOU	

Action

In the same game as above you lose an all-in and find yourself down to 17.5 big blinds a few hands later. You are dealt 2-2 in the small blind. Do you a) fold, b) call, c) raise to 600 or d) move all-in?

Answer

d) move all-in. Although you have over 15 big blinds here 22 will almost never be ahead if you raise then have to call an all-in and if your opponent calls it will be difficult to play postflop unless you hit a set. You are well within the maximum stack size for moving all-in with 2-2 to be profitable, so this is a good time to revert to an all-in strategy with a deeper stack.

9. Playing against a loose-passive opponent

Game: $5 9-player turbo sitngo

Players left: 2

Hand: 10♣-7♠

Position: Small Blind

Blinds: 100/200/a25

Stacks:

SB	BB
7000	6500
YOU	

Action

You are heads-up with a loose-passive player who plays poorly postflop and are dealt 10-7o. Do you a) fold, b) call, c) raise to 600 or d) move all-in?

Answer

a) call. Against this player you should aim to play smallball to avoid risking significant amounts of chips without a hand, and try to exploit your positional and postflop advantages. Calling here is therefore ideal as you will usually get to see a flop cheaply and can proceed from there, extracting value if you catch anything and checking it down or bluffing when appropriate if not.

10. Facing a raise with deep stacks

Game:	$55 9-player turbo sitngo
Players left:	2
Hand:	A♣-2♠
Position:	Big Blind
Blinds:	100/200/a25
Stacks:	

SB	BB
9000	4500
	YOU

Action

You are heads-up with 22.5 big blinds and are dealt A-2o. The loose-aggressive small blind opens to 600. Do you a) fold, b) call c) raise to 1800 or d) move all-in?

Answer

d) move all-in. Although you will usually be behind when called, an ace is a massive hand heads-up against a loose opener and you need to accumulate chips wherever possible. The 850 chips on offer in the pot will easily compensate for the times you are called and behind, and you may even be called by hands like K-Q or K-J and be ahead.

Non-standard sitngos

1. Playing a draw early in a six-max sitngo

Game: $210 6-player turbo sitngo

Players left: 6

Hand: A♠-7♠

Position: Button

Blinds: 10/20

Stacks:

UTG	+1	CO	Button	SB	BB
1470	1530	1500	1500	1500	1500
			YOU		

Action

Early on in a six-max sitngo you raise to 80 on the button with A♠-7♠ and are called in the big blind by a loose-aggressive player. The flop comes 8♠-9♠-2♣ and you continuation bet for 120 after your opponent checks, but he check-raises to 340. Do you a) fold, b) call or c) move all-in?

Answer

c) move all-in. Although you will usually lose equity when you are called, in this format you should play to accumulate chips, and it is by no means certain that your opponent will be committing to the hand. Playing aggressively will allow you to increase your stack without a showdown some of the time here, and also balances the times you have a very big hand like aces or kings and play the same way.

2. Playing a dominating stack on the bubble of a six-max sitngo

Game:	$25 6-player turbo sitngo
Players left:	3
Hand:	3♣-2♠
Position:	Button
Blinds:	120/240
Stacks:	

Button	SB	BB
6000	1500	1500
YOU		

Action

You have a dominating chip lead in a six-max sitngo with a standard 65%/35% payout structure and are up against two competent players. You are dealt 3-2o first to act. Do you a) fold. b) call or c) move all-in?

Answer

c) move all-in. Because of the high payout awarded to second place, this will be a +$EV move according to ICM if your opponents only call with the top 17% of all hands (3-3+, A-7o+, A-2s+, K-Qo, K-10s+), which will usually be the case against competent opposition. You should therefore be looking to move all-in with almost every hand at this stage in order to accumulate as many chips as possible whilst your opponents play for second, until one of them is committed in the big blind.

3. Playing the middle stack on the bubble of a six-max sitngo

Game:	$5 6-player turbo sitngo
Players left:	3
Hand:	A♦-Q♦
Position:	Big Blind
Blinds:	120/240
Stacks:	

Button	SB	BB
4800	1500	2700
		YOU

Action

You are in second place on the bubble of a $5 six-max turbo with A-Qo on the big blind. The button raises all-in and the small blind folds. Do you a) fold or b) call?

Answer

a) fold. Although calling with A-Qo would be fractionally +$EV according to ICM if your opponent was pushing 100% of the time, at this level you cannot be sure he will use this strategy and therefore you should fold and avoid making a big error which would give the small blind a chance of advancing to second place.

4. Playing a marginal hand on the bubble of a two-table sitngo

Game:	$50 20-player turbo sitngo
Players left:	5
Hand:	A♥-9♣
Position:	UTG
Blinds:	300/600/a50
Stacks:	

UTG	CO	Button	SB	BB
6000	6000	6000	6000	6000
YOU				

Action

You are on the bubble of a two table sitngo with a standard 40%/30%/20%/10% payout and have been dealt A-9o under-the-gun. Do you a) fold, b) call, c) raise to 1800 or d) move all-in?

Answer

a) fold. With several players still to act behind you and a flat payout structure, you are best off trying to avoid unnecessary risks and move up the money when other players get all-in, rather that trying to accumulate a dominating stack. Here your opponents would have to call with only the top 4% of all hands (10-10+, A-Q+) for this to be profitable according to ICM, and against so many opponents this is unlikely to be the case.

5. Facing a tough decision on the bubble of a satellite

Game: $80 10-player satellite to $200 tournament (four seats)

Players left: 5

Hand: J♠-J♦

Position: Big Blind

Blinds: 150/300

Stacks:

UTG	CO	Button	SB	BB
3000	3000	3000	3000	3000
				YOU

Action

You are in the big blind on the bubble of a satellite to a larger online tournament with J-J when everyone folds to the small blind who moves all-in. Do you a) fold or b) call?

Answer

a) fold. Although jacks are a big hand to fold here, you would need to be very sure of winning to call as you are essentially creating a freeroll for the other players into the main tournament. If you fold your equity will be $153.16 whilst if you call you will either win a $200 seat or be eliminated with nothing, meaning that you need to be at least a 76.58% favourite against his range according to ICM. Jacks have 77.47% equity against a random hand, but you would have to be 100% sure he was moving all-in every time here to consider calling, and even then you may be better off folding if other players are likely to make foolish mistakes that would benefit you on subsequent hands. Your opponent's pushing range is key here, for example even with K-K it would still be correct to fold if he was moving all-in with 20% or less of hands.

6. Playing when someone is all-in on the bubble in a satellite

Game:	$80 10-player satellite to $200 tournament (four seats)
Players left:	5
Hand:	A♠-A♦
Position:	Button
Blinds:	200/400/a25
Stacks:	

UTG	CO	Button	SB	BB
3600	3000	5000	3000	400
		YOU		

Action

You are the chip leader on the bubble of a satellite to a large online tournament and there is a player all-in in the big blind. The first two players limp in front of you and you have aces on the button. Do you a) fold, b) call, c) raise to 1200 or d) move all-in?

Answer

b) call. Although you have been dealt aces you should still play to create the best possible chance of the big blind being eliminated here, as you do not get any reward for the number of chips you finish the tournament with. Raising would actually give the big blind a better chance of survival if you force the other players out, which would in turn reduce your $EV, and therefore calling and checking the hand down is the best strategy at this point.